Church of Christ
at Whispering Hills

Our History 2002-2018

21349 E 111th ST
Broken Arrow, Oklahoma 74014

James Kay Publishing

Tulsa, Oklahoma

Church of Christ at Whispering Hills
Our History 2002-2018

ISBN 978-1-943245-30-7

www.jameskaypublishing.com

e-mail: sales@jameskaypublishing.com

Photos Provided by Church of Christ at Whispering Hills

1.2 bw

Dedication

This history is dedicated to those charter members who worked so
hard to establish a truth seeking, loving congregation:

Doug & Cathy Aitkenhead
Evelyn Barthel
Stephen Bates
Nathan & Pam Bell
Lawrence & Barbara Buckner
Margaret Campbell
Charles & Lynda Chase
Rod & Lisa Copelin, Ashley, Levi, Hunter
Bill & Joy Ellis
Verlin Embry
Jeane Freeman
Jesse & Sheryl Guiterres
Earl & Jan Laney
Glen & Winnie Matthews, August Rain
Roger & Myra Matthews, Rodney
Charles & Rae Parette
Roy & Kathryn Priest
Eric & Amy Putman
Everett & Letha Putman
Ed & Martha Rentie, Joe
Walter & Regina Sorrell
Jerry & Diana Spradley
Bob & Ida Stover
Collin Teakell
Grant Teakell
Kevin Teakell
Russell & Margaret Teakell
Russell & Terri Wadsworth
Craig Wooten
Geames & Lori Wooten

Church of Christ at Whispering Hills

First Worship Service
September 1, 2002

From Our Elders

September 1, 2018

Greetings to all the past and current members of the Church of Christ at Whispering Hills in Broken Arrow, Oklahoma. The Lord has blessed us in so many ways during our short history as a congregation. The facility has provided us with comfort, security, and a meeting place for the community. The land that was donated has been a true blessing and has been utilized to spread God's Word.

We are indebted to those fine Christian families who were the original members, that sacrificed and served to ensure that the Lord's church would be planted and nourished at the current location over the ensuing years. A special appreciation to Geames Wooten, Nathan Bell, and Jerry Spradley who were the original elders.

The congregation has also been blessed by the service of additional elders and deacons who have contributed to the management and growth of the brotherhood. To our peaceful and spiritual Lord's church, we can only say, "Thank You".

For the future at Whispering Hills we pray that we will continue to follow and practice New Testament principles that will have an impact for our Lord and Savior Jesus Christ in the community in which we live and work. May we always speak the "Truth in Love".

Wayne Ford

Steve Parrott

Tony Lightsey

Mike Snider

Our Elders

Wayne Ford (2015 - Present)

Tony Lightsey (2010 - Present)

Steve Parrott (2010 - Present)

Mike Snider (2007 - Present)

Foreword

It has been a joy to work on this history, and I appreciate the help and comments that several of the congregation have given. Of course, no true history of the Church of Christ at Whispering Hills would be complete without the beginning history of the Church of Christ in Broken Arrow, Oklahoma.

The Broken Arrow Church of Christ possibly had a beginning as early as 1917 or 1918. The 1909 Census had two people listed as members of the churches of Christ. A. G. Murphy moved to Broken Arrow in 1917 and was a leader in the congregation in its early years. Also, Charlie and Ona Snelson came to Broken Arrow in 1918. Their late son, Ray, told that men of the congregation would read scripture and make a few comments since they had no located minister. The late **Gertrude King, an ancestor of Joyce Foster** and **Bill Lundy**, said her parents moved to Broken Arrow in 1921 and people were already meeting in a public place in 1922 or 1923. Other Whispering Hills members who have their religious roots back to the early days of the church in Broken Arrow are descendants of A. C. and Mary Key whose great grandsons, **Allen and Mark Messick**, and Mark's two granddaughters, **Drew** and **Ryan Morris**; Marion and Della Johnston, grandparents of **Winnie Cotner Matthews, deceased wife of Glen**, and **Delores Watson Wilson**. Another early member of the church in Broken Arrow was **Earl Laney's** stepmother, Oleta Laney, daughter of Eschal Helm. **Margaret Campbell** also grew up in the Broken Arrow Church of Christ. When the Elders first asked me to do this, I knew it would be a big undertaking. Please forgive me if you don't see pictures and items listed that you would have liked. I have asked for information, pictures, etc. Anyway, it's time for me to put it to an end; so maybe this will be a beginning for someone to build upon.

What a heritage we have at Whispering Hills!

Lori Wooten

Acknowledgments

It is impossible to acknowledge everyone who has contributed to the History of the Church of Christ of Whispering Hills. Thanks to those who have supplied pictures, encouragement, information, etc. Several pictures and early information obtained from family of Winnie Matthews, deceased wife of Glen.

A special thanks to the following who have made significant contributions to this work:

Clif Dreiling

Dale Graham

Deborah Houston

Rae Parette

Thanks also to those who have supplied pictures, encouragement, etc.

Who We Are

The Church of Christ at Whispering Hills is not a denomination, nor are we interdenominational (I Corinthians 1.10-13). We are simply a local group of Christians (I Corinthians 1.2; Acts 11.26; I Peter 1.22-25) who meet together to worship the Lord (Acts 20.7) and do God's work together (Acts 8.4; James 1.27). We follow no human creeds or doctrines (Matthew 15.8-9; 2 John 9; Revelation 22.18-19), but follow Christ through His word (Ephesians 1.22-23; 2 Timothy 3.16-17. We gladly provide scriptural authority for all we believe, teach and do (Colossians 3.17). Our worship is not after human traditions but is in spirit and truth (John 4.23-24). Members of the Church of Christ at Whispering Hills are expected to live godly lives, exemplary of Christ. Our hope is a home in Heaven.

Our mission at Whispering Hills is to change lives through Jesus Christ:

- As you sing God's praises, may you be invigorated by His power and glory.

- As you listen to His Word, may you humbly obey and receive His life giving truth.

- As you commune with Him in prayer and around His table, may you be intimately reminded that he loves you and gave Himself for you.

- As you fellowship with His children, may you be encouraged to be crucified with Christ, and to live your life by faith in the Son of God.

Table of Contents

Table of Contents

Table of Contents

Table of Contents

Church of Christ at Whispering Hills

Broken Arrow, Oklahoma

Section One

History

BROKEN ARROW CHURCH OF CHRIST

1920s

Broken Arrow was just leaving her teen years when the Church of Christ emerged here. Farmers were coming into town with their belongings in covered wagons, spending the night in the wagon yard then driving out to leased or newly purchased land. Some sent their women, younger children and household goods here by train while the men and older boys came by wagon with the livestock. Some rented rail cars and brought family, furniture, farm equipment and livestock in by rail. This was a young country with rich prairie land. Others came here to set up businesses or work in the coal mines.

Among these new settlers were a few church members. Although the 1909 religious census listed the number of Church of Christ members as two, it was not until the early 1920s that any recorded effort was made to get the church established here. Three families, the A. C. Keys (great grandparents of Allen and Mark Messick), the Musgroves, and a brother Bradshaw began meeting together in the home of Brother and Sister Musgove on East College Street. Since there was no regular preacher, the men would read scripture and make a few comments.

A. C. and Mary Key

Shortly after the home meetings began, Brother Key sent for Brother W. E. "Joe" Warlick to come for a meeting. He helped the church get organized to meet for worship. The church then rented a room above the jail in the old City Hall, a block east of Main on Dallas. A. G. Murphy preached the first sermon in the rented room. This room also served as Judge Walton's court room and as a meeting place for the Odd Fellows, the National Guard, and the City Library.

Ruby Messick, daughter of the Keys says that baptisms were held in Haskell Pond. She noted that families in the early church here each owned their own song books and brought them with them to worship. She also said that each person went to the front of the room to be served the Lord's Supper and left contributions there also.

Every Sunday the church had to set up the chairs and communion table. [Sounds familiar doesn't it.] Several people told that Brother Key took the ridicule of the street loafers as he carried the communion emblems to and from the building in a small picnic-like basket covered with a cloth. He ignored them and took care of the communion for many years.

Those on record who met in that upper room were these families: A. C. and Mary Matilda Key, Robert P. and Agee King, Escal and Emma Helm, Arthur "A. G." and Bertha Murphy, Della Johnston, George and Jessie Lemon, John and Hattie Blythe, Bill and Lucinda Blythe and Mrs. Gasset and her son. [The underscored people have descendants who are members of Whispering Hills.]

Brother A. C. Key was one of the establishers and sustainers of the church here. He opened a shoe repair shop on Main Street, added a hardware store and had a tombstone cutter. He and his family lived in eight rooms over the store, which was located in the present Kemp Hardware. The Keys lived there until the late 1940s.

> Bea Johnston Dougan Stackhouse compiled information on the Keys from memory: One could buy farm supplies, nails, hammers, hardware, leather, dishes, harness and anything you asked for and if he didn't have it he would order it if it was available. In the store stood a wooden full-grown horse, harness and all. [Presently located in the Broken Arrow Museum and previously in the lobby of Arkansas Valley Bank.] It intrigued us kids every time we went in which was every Saturday because Brother Key was also a shoe cobbler, and with five children, Dad usually had a pair of shoes to be mended.

> One thing was very prevalent in the store and that was Brother Key's open Bible on the counter. When customers came in he always took time to talk of God's Word and invite them to worship.

> There was no church building because there were only two families who were members of the church who took turns meeting in each other's houses for worship. Brother Key began talking to my Dad (F. Marion Johnston) that summer and told him that he had a young preacher coming for a gospel meeting that would run two weeks under a tent on a lot close to the store. That preacher was R. A. Hartsell, then 18 years old. Brother Key told my dad, "You'll have to come hear this boy preacher, he is dynamic." Brother Key paid for the meeting himself.

> Well, Dad promised he'd come and our family went the first night. Dad fell in love with that boy Hartsell. We went every night and my Dad was baptized. Mama was already a member having been baptized by Brother Murphy one summer at Weer. Her dad and mother were members of the church in Missouri and Grandad Cox was an elder there. They came to Oklahoma before statehood by wagon train. Mama was seven years old then.

4

After the meeting, there were enough people that Brother Key rented the City Hall and started the church. One family came in a wagon as they lived way out in the country – they were the Whites, already members of the church. They would stay all day so they could be at worship Sunday evening. They brought their lunch which consisted of fried salt pork and biscuits. Such devotion to God seldom is found.

The first Lord's Day there were about 30 people, the Keys, the Kings, the Johnstons and two other families. If it had not been for this wonderful man, A. C. Key, his hardware store and his devotion to his God and the church, our family might never have known the Way of Salvation. He was the "Key" that opened the door of truth for us. He was a cobbler.

The times were hard and most men were farmers. They often brought farm produce, fruit, chickens, and hog meat to give to the preachers because they didn't make much of a salary.

Sister Stackhouse also has several memories of her own family. She says the Johnston house was a place where preachers and family stayed when in meetings or while waiting for a place to live when they were hired as local ministers. She writes:

I don't remember a Sunday when we didn't have a house full of company from church for dinner and supper. Dad always asked the preacher and family and anyone else he thought needed a good meal. Mama always had enough food no matter how many were there. I have seen her run out in the yard and grab a frying chicken and have it dressed and cooked in time for the second table when she saw the three chickens she had already prepared were almost gone at the first table. She could whip up a meal if unexpected guests came. She could take a can of salmon and a box of crackers and eggs and feed a multitude. She made pies, cakes and baked loaves of bread. She always had canned goods from her garden and potatoes from they grew on the farm. If ever there was a hospitality house, it was my mother and dad's and they loved it.

- Recollection from Bea Johnston Dougan Stackhouse

F. Marion & Della Johnston

Another pioneer family in the early history of the church in Broken Arrow was the F. Marion and Della Johnston family. Marion moved to Broken Arrow in the 1920s from Arkansas. Della moved with her family from Missouri. The property on which our congregation meets is land they homesteaded in the 1920s. Della was baptized by A. G. Murphy one summer at Weer; and Marion was baptized in the meeting by R. A. Hartsel, previously mentioned.

After worship on Sundays found Della preparing "Sunday Dinner" for all the members who could come. While some were eating, she could be found in the chicken house wringing the necks of chickens so there would be enough to eat. She never knew how many would come and no one ever went away hungry!

F. Marion and Della Johnston Homeplace
(Property of John and Deanie Casey which borders
previous home of Geames & Lori Wooten)

Another person who was baptized in the meeting of 1924 was **Henderson King**, husband of Gertrude. Gertrude had been baptized at age 16, in a mill pond in Arkansas. "We had what was called protracted meetings in those days." She told an interviewer several years ago, "When enough interest was aroused, they would just keep extending the meeting as long as they felt some good was being done." Sister King never forgot one evening of that meeting. as they were returning home in their horse and buggy, when right along beside the cemetery, the horse stumbled causing the buggy to jolt. "Kelsa (their one year old son) fell out of my lap and under the buggy and one of the wheels ran over him. We just picked him up and felt of him. He didn't have any broken bones and didn't seem to be hurt, so we just came home and went to bed.

Henderson and Gertrude King, and Henderson's parents (Robert Polk and Agee Luvinia Ridgway King) and family, came here from Arkansas in November 1921 in two covered wagons. They chartered a railroad car to bring their belongings here. The families spent the first night, a cold gloomy night, in the wagon yard! Children of Agee and Robert were Cleora Robertson, John Almus King, Annie Perry, Henderson King, Cuba Luther, Vada Finley, Herman Byran King, Heber King, Veah Draper, Hatler King, and Robert Emerson King. Two grandchildren of Robert P. and Agee King, Joyce Foster and Bill Lundy, worship with us here.

Robert P. King was a lumberman, farmer, stockman, and maker of sorghum molasses. His son Henderson took over making molasses when his dad died. R. P. didn't believe in paying a preacher. He said a preacher should "work by the sweat of his brow." R. P. King's granddaughter, Joyce Foster, said that he was a kind, gentle man.

Robert P. & Agee King

Gertrude King said her mother-in-law was an especially strong Christian woman, and she was the last one to leave the church building. Gertrude patterned her Christianity after her mother-in-law and her mother, Fanny Perry. Gertrude said that the church was already meeting here in Broken Arrow when they came in late 1921. The King families moved to farms southwest of Broken Arrow. The summer of 1922, they started meeting with the church in town. Gertrude noted that the men of the congregation read scriptures, gave talks, and taught lessons.

Around 1919, **Ezra and Dora Cotner** came with their three children, Velma, Raymond, and Herman. They had been traveling for over a year in a covered wagon. Leaving Chishomville, Arkansas, to find a better place to live in Colorado. They found that was not what they wanted, so were heading back home to Arkansas. They were camping out here in Broken Arrow. A young boy saw their nice pair of mules and told his dad to come see them. When the farmer saw them, he asked Mr. Cotner to be his share cropper. Mr. Cotner thought he wanted to go home, so they started for Arkansas. They came to a cross-road, one leading to home and the other leading back to Broken Arrow. Raymond remembered the three children peeking from under the buckboard seat, wondering which way they would go. They wanted to stay here to see what this area was like. Mrs. Cotner was tired and weary of the long trip and for once, went against her husband by taking hold of the reins and turning the team of mules in the direction of Broken Arrow. They settled here and farmed. Raymond and Herman were very young boys, approximately nine and seven years of age. In their teen years, they began attending worship services to see the young girls. Raymond's eye was on Vera Johnston. They were sweethearts in school. Later, Herman met his bride, Pauline "Polly" Moore, daughter of Mr. and Mrs. Guy Moore (both were converted to Christ as adults after coming to Broken Arrow.) Raymond and Herman served as elders, and their families were a big influence. Raymond and Vera Johnston Cotner were the parents of Winnie Cotner Matthews.

[Ask Bill when his grandfather, John, came to BA]

Fred Lundy's father, John, invited Charles C. Fuqua to hold a meeting. The elder Lundy, Stockard Lee and Brother Harlan (who lived in Owasso and attended Broken Arrow) helped pay Fuqua's bus fare. John W. Lundy, his wife, Myrtle, and their children were here in the 1920s, but went to Bixby for a time. They came back around 1936. Their children are Lollie, Lloyd, Norman, Violet, Carl, John Jr., Fred, Edna, and Ora Faye. Fred Lundy remembers being baptized on March 14, 1937 by Brother A. G. Murphy. Fred and Billie June King, previously mentioned were the parents of our Bill Lundy. It is interesting to note that some of those of our congregation who have ties to these early Christians, have both maternal and paternal ancestors who were among the earliest members of the church in Broken Arrow. Again, what a heritage!

Many other families were involved in the early days of the church in Broken Arrow, but I have primarily mentioned the ones with connections to Whispering Hills.

Broken Arrow Church of Christ
Ash and Broadway
1927 - 1949

Margaret Campbell Remembers:

In 1927, the Broken Arrow Church of Christ purchased the old red brick Methodist Church building at Ash and Broadway. It was built in 1905 and now is the current Windstream building. 1943 was the first time Margaret Campbell was in the old red brick building as her grandfather, Lucas Woodward, died and they had his funeral there.

In 1946, Margaret's family moved from 71st and Evans Road to 104th and Lynn Lane Road. No more muddy roads to get out of Wagoner County! In 1948, they were able to go to church full time. She remembers the steeple, pigeons and the baptistry. It was a very pretty building.

In 1949, men started tearing down the red brick building. Many families including Margaret's met at night to clean up the site. Women scraped bricks and the children would stack them; the men did the heavy work. I saw Earl Laney on the dozer. March 13, 1949.

On October 2, 1949, Margaret was the first person to be baptized by Ben Adams, Minister. After this time, the minister, Ben Adams, was going to baptize one of the young men, Lonnie Smithson, who was 6 feet tall. As he lowered him into the water, he banged his head on the wall of the baptistry

First Church of Christ VBS in Broken Arrow

Can you find three of our members: Winnie Cotner Matthews,
Deceased; Margaret Ogle Campbell; and Joyce Finley Foster?

**Winnie Cotner Matthews, deceased,
and Margaret Ogle Campbell**

How It All Began

This is an easy story to tell because it shows how love for the Lord, God's providence, and determination can build a congregation of God's people. Around 1981, about 37 years ago, the Elders of the Broken Arrow Church of Christ dreamed of establishing another congregation in the South part of Broken Arrow. This became a reality on September 1, 2002, when a group of approximately 55 members from the Broken Arrow Church of Christ met for the first time as the Church of Christ at Whispering Hills. We met in the Broken Arrow Senior Citizens Center at 1600 S. Main, Broken Arrow, OK. Kelly Riggs from the Broken Arrow congregation was our first speaker with Herschel Dyer as our second. We had a total of 106 people in attendance and a contribution of $2,358.04.

Geames & Lori Wooten began visiting Bea Johnston Dougan and Dan Stackhouse in 1993, shortly after building a new home on 209th E Avenue. This property had originally been part of the land homesteaded by Bea's father, Marion Johnston. They were needing a place to keep their horses and asked if the Stackhouses would be interested in selling or leasing their property. They said "no," but they could use the property as their own. So Geames built a barn and used it for his horses. This property along with their home, John & Deanie Casey's, and the church property were part of the half section of land homesteaded by F. Marion and Della Johnston. Winnie Cotner Matthews, deceased wife of Glen, and Delores Watson Wilson, were granddaughters of the Johnstons. All of the homes from two houses North of the bridge on 209th to 111th Street South were members of the church and 209th E Ave was "called" by many, "Church of Christ Lane." Also, at one time there were five members of the Broken Arrow congregation, who served as Elders who owned property on 209th E Ave.

The Wootens visited the Stackhouses several times before Bea mentioned sometime in 1999, that she wanted to donate 20 acres of land for the purpose of building a new congregation on her daddy's land. It seems that had always been a dream of hers. As Geames was an Elder of the Broken Arrow congregation at the time, he felt it was better for the Stackhouses to deed the land to the church at Broken Arrow. On July 24, 2000, the Stackhouses wrote a letter to the Broken Arrow Elders expressing their desire to donate their 20 acres for a new congregation.

On August 27, 2000, Bill Rampey, one of the Broken Arrow Elders, now deceased, made the announcement before the morning worship about the wonderful opportunity that the new congregation would be for the South part of Broken Arrow and the Wagoner County area.

Your word is a lamp to my feet and a light for my path.

Ps 119:105

July 24, 2000

Church of Christ
ATTN: The Elders
811 North 4th Street
Broken Arrow, Oklahoma 74012

Dear Brethren:

This is to advise you that we plan to give to your congregation twenty (20) acres of land. Ten (10) acres to be donated this year of 2000 and ten (10) acres to be donated in the year of 2001.

This land is for the purpose of establishing a congregation of the Lord's people. The building will be as you desire.

This land is not to be sold for any reason, but retained for the church use only, later you may wish to establish a care
home for elderly or disabled members. This is at your discretion.

This land is given in remembrance of MR. & MRS. MARION & DELLA JOHNSTON, MARION was a former elder, also in memory of VERSAL L. JOHNSTON & PAUL F. JOHNSTON who were faithful gospel preachers. Our names, DAN & BEA STACKHOUSE are not to be announced regarding this gift.

There are some consideration we desire regarding the congregation you establish on this land, and we would like this incorporated in the charter. This is covered in other Church of Christ charters.

1. The Holy Scriptures shall be taught and accepted as the final, all-sufficient revelation from God to man, and regarded as an infallible rule of faith and practice.

2. Mechanical instruments of music shall never be permitted to be brought on to the premises, for the purpose of being used in worship, or for any other purpose, use or design.

3. No teacher or preacher shall be allowed use of the building, its premises, and grounds for the purpose of advocating any doctrine or practice which conflicts with the teaching and practice of the church of Christ as taught in the Bible and as currently held by the elders, trustees, or members responsible for the execution of this charter. Expressly excluded from such use are any and all teachers, preachers and others who hold to any form of liberalism, modernism, or premillennialism, along with all hobby-riders, factionists and divisive persons, who advocate any doctrine or practice in conflict with the teaching and practice now current in the churches of Christ.

It is not our intent to tell you what to do regarding the charter, but our prayers and hope is for a strong congregation
of the Lord's people to be established on this land.

In Christian love,

Dan Stackhouse

Bea Stackhouse

Hearts Turning Home

Broken Arrow Church of Christ   "Touching the Heart of Our Community"

505 E. Kenosha   Broken Arrow, OK 74012   (918) 258-9602   Fax (918) 258-9604   www.bacoc.org   info@bacoc.org

ELDERS:

Bill Duwe
Kendall Dykes
Charles Emerson
Dave Larson
Jim Lee
Gerry Lynn
James Parker
Jim Parker
Geames Wooten

MINISTERS:

Dr. Bill Keele
Scott Keele
Rich Dolan
Wayne Pope

February 14, 2002

Dear Brothers and Sisters in Christ:

The elders want to give you insight into our discussions concerning the 111th property. The property, with restrictions, was given to our congregation for the purpose of expanding the Lord's church in this area. During our 2001 planning session we developed a long-range plan and the first year of the plan, which was 2001, has been completed. Goals in the years beyond 2002 could change as the project develops.

Long Range Plan

2001	Develop a possible site plan
2002	Form an evangelistic support group
2003	Evangelist minister
2004	Year of development
2005	Help fund site development if required
2007	Church meeting on the property

Our commitment is to treat the 111th property as a mission point and do what we can to see that the project is successful. Since the property is close to our building and since some of our members will be involved to a greater degree than our usual mission points, we feel some statements of understanding need to be made.

111th Property Statements of Understanding

- Do what we can to ensure the establishment of a doctrinally sound church on the property.

- Do what we can to keep the establishment of the church on the 111th property from being perceived as a "split" from the BA congregation.

- Encourage those who express interest in the project, regardless of their present Church of Christ membership.

- We will not be the oversight eldership of the 111th congregation.

- We will retain ownership of the property until an appropriate time and condition of transfer exists

- We will encourage the new congregation to make plans for expansion into a congregation of 2000 or more members because the site will accommodate a large congregation.

- We will remain committed to providing the best possible opportunity for spiritual and numeric growth at our present location while helping a church become established on the 111th property.

- We encourage and will support the establishment of a Bible chair on the 111th property. The new university is growing and establishment of a Bible chair is important.

- Funding and other services by the BA congregation will be handled as we currently administer assistance for any mission work.

- Members or staff from our congregation who work on the 111th project will be considered as members in good standing and performing a local mission effort.

For the elders,

Gerry Lynn

During the Elders Planning Session in February 2001, one item on the agenda was to begin planning for the new congregation; so long-range plans for the property, which is now Whispering Hills, began.

In January 2002, a group was formed at the Broken Arrow congregation to begin planning for the new congregation. The group was Take-a-City #8. "Take-a-City" is a state-side mission work of the Broken Arrow congregation to help small U.S. congregations. Some of the members of the TAC Group 8 committed themselves to become charter members of the Church of Christ at Whispering Hills in order to further evangelize the Broken Arrow community and the surrounding area through the avenue of this new congregation in South Broken Arrow.

A letter was sent out to the Broken Arrow congregation, written by Gerry Lynn for the Elders February 14, 2002, to form an evangelistic support group and that a minister would be hired in 2003. Because of this, the plans for a new congregation began a lot sooner than originally planned. Whispering Hills began as a congregation September 1, 2002, in the Senior Citizens Center at 1800 S. Main Street, and continued meeting there until our building was completed June 6, 2004.

The donors of the land were present at our first meeting as a congregation, and they were also present for our first Worship Service in the building at the present location on June 6, 2004.

Take-a-City #8

Families who were part of this TAC Group 8 were:

Doug Aitkenheads, Nathan Bells, Adam Brewers, Lawrence Buckners, Margaret Campbell, Verlin Embrey, Jess & Sheryl Guiterres', Jack Hales, Allen Marshalls, Glen Matthews, Charles Parettes, Dick Rays, Walter Sorrells, Jerry Spradleys, Bob Stovers, Russell Wadsworths, Jim Waltons, and Geames Wootens. They formed a steering committee and had meetings regularly.

Members of TAC #8 met once a month after evening services at the Broken Arrow congregation and met a few times in homes. One of these events was an out-door fellowship held at Glen and Winnie Matthews' home on South Lynn Lane.

TAC #8 Fellowship
at Glen & Winnie Matthews'

Adam & Tammy Brewer, Charles
Parette, Margaret Campbell

Geames Wooten, Jack & Gloria Hale

Kirk Maupin, Jerry & Diana Spradley,
Patti Maupin, Richard Holleyman

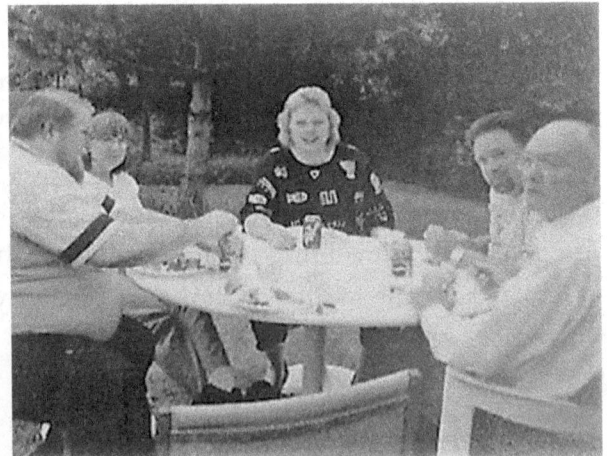

Russell & Margaret Teakell, Pam & Nathan Bell, Glen Matthews

CERTIFICATE OF INCORPORATION

A NOT FOR PROFIT CORPORATION

TO THE SECRETARY OF STATE OF THE STATE OF OKLAHOMA:

KNOW ALL MEN BY THESE PRESENTS:

That we, whose names are hereunto subscribed, do hereby associate our-selves together for the purpose of forming a religious not for profit corporation under the provisions of the corporation laws of the State of Oklahoma, and for that purpose state:

ARTICLES

I

The name of the corporation is: Church Of Christ At Whispering Hills, Inc.

II

The address of the corporation's registered office in the State of Oklahoma is:

21349 East 111th Street South, Broken Arrow, Wagoner County, Oklaho-ma 74014, and the name of its registered agent is Geames Wooten.

III

The future location of the church edifice is:

21349 East 111th Street South, Broken Arrow, Wagoner County, Oklaho-ma 74014.

IV

The duration of the corporation is: Perpetual.

V

This religious not for profit corporation does not have the authority to issue capi-tal stock.

Mailing Address: James King
_____1111 North Fourth Street
_____Broken Arrow, OK 74012

No.Doc. Stamps
68 O.S. 3201(3)

QUIT-CLAIM DEED

THIS INDENTURE made this *12* day of *December*, 2002, between **Broken Arrow Church of Christ, aka The Church of Christ of Broken Arrow, Oklahoma, an Oklahoma Corporation**, party of the first part, hereinafter called Grantor, and **Church of Christ at Whispering Hills, Inc.**, party of the second part, hereinafter called Grantee.

WITNESSETH, that in consideration of the sum of TEN AND NO/100 DOLLARS ($10.00), and other good and valuable consideration, the receipt and sufficiency of which is hereby acknowledged, Grantor does, by these presents, grant, bargain, sell, convey and quit-claim unto said Grantee, its successors and assigns, all of its right, title, interest and estate, both at law and in equity of, in and to the following described real estate, situated in the County of Wagoner, State of Oklahoma, to-wit:

The West Half of the Southeast Quarter of the Southwest Quarter (W/2 SE/4 SW/4) of Section Twenty-Nine (29), Township Eighteen (18) North, Range Fifteen (15) East, Wagoner County, State of Oklahoma

together with all the improvements thereon and appurtenances thereunto belonging.

TO HAVE AND TO HOLD said described premises unto said party Grantee, its successors and assigns forever.

IN WITNESS WHEREOF, the said Grantor caused these presents to be signed in its name, the year and day first above written.

Broken Arrow Church of Christ, aka
The Church of Christ of Broken Arrow, Oklahoma

Dave Larson
_____
Dave Larson, President

STATE OF OKLAHOMA)
)ss.   **ACKNOWLEDGMENT**
COUNTY OF TULSA   )

BEFORE ME, the undersigned, a Notary Public, in and for said County and State, on this *12* day of *December*, 2002, personally appeared Dave Larson, in his capacity as the President of Broken Arrow Church of Christ, aka The Church of Christ of Broken Arrow, Oklahoma, an Oklahoma Corporation, known to me to be the same in said capacity, who executed the within and foregoing instrument and acknowledged to me that he executed the same as his free and voluntary act and deed and as the free and voluntary act and deed of such corporation, for the uses and purposes therein set forth.

GIVEN under my hand and seal the day and year above written.

Rebecca Cox
_____
Notary Public

My Commission expires:

Rebecca Cox
Comm #00010332
Exp. Date 07-18-04

18

BY-LAWS
OF
THE CHURCH OF CHRIST
AT WHISPERING HILLS

ARTICLE I

Section 1: The name of this corporation shall be "The Church of Christ At Whispering Hills, Inc.".

Section 2: Its principal office shall be located at 21349 East 111th St. South, Broken Arrow, Wagoner County, State of Oklahoma 74014.

ARTICLE II

Section 1: All members of the congregation in good and regular standing shall be members of this corporation. Only the Board of Trustees shall be entitled to vote in any regular or special meeting.

ARTICLE III

Section 1: There shall be an annual meeting of the corporation on the second Monday of January in each year at the principal office of the corporation, at which time no more than eleven Trustees shall be selected from the membership, and any business properly coming before such meeting may be transacted.

Section 2: Special meetings of the members of this corporation, otherwise known as the congregation, shall be held at the same place as the annual; meeting and may be called at any time, by the President, and in his absence, by another member of the Board of Trustees.

Section 3: Notice of the time and place of all annual and special meetings shall be given by the Board of Trustees by announcement from the pulpit at least seven days prior to the meeting and shall post a copy of such notice in the church bulletin or paper.

Section 4: The President of the corporation, or in his absence, the Vice-President shall preside at all such meetings.

Section 5: At every such meeting each Trustee shall be entitled to cast one vote.

Section 6: A quorum for the transaction of business at any such meeting shall consist of a majority of the Trustees in attendance who are in good and regular standing.

Section 7: Trustees shall have power by a majority vote at any such meeting to remove any Trustee from office.

ARTICLE IV

Section 1: The business and property of the corporation shall be managed by three Officer-Trustees, preferably elders, deacons or both, who shall be selected by the Trustees. The Officer-Trustees shall not purchase, sell or encumber real or personal property or purchase and sell stock, bonds or debentures, or construct or refurbish the corporate property of the congregation unless they do so by a vote of the majority of the Trustees of the congregation.

Section 2: The Board of Trustees and Officer-Trustees, with the exception of elders, shall be elected for a term of one year and shall hold office until succeeding Trustees are elected on the second Monday of January of each year. However, the number of terms of office of any Trustee shall not be limited.

Section 3: The regular meeting of the Trustees shall be held in the office of the corporation immediately after the adjournment of the annual corporation meeting.

Section 4: Special meetings of the Board of Trustees shall be held in the principal office of the corporation and may be called by the President, and in his absence, by the Vice President.

Section 5: Vacancies in the Board of Trustees may be filled by a majority vote of the Trustees at any regular or special meeting.

Section 6: The Trustees shall submit a statement of the business performed during the preceding year, together with a general financial statement of the corporation, along with proposed plans for the future of the corporation.

ARTICLE V

Section 1: The Officers of this corporation shall be a President, Vice President, Secretary and Treasurer who shall be elected for a term of one year and shall hold office until their successors are duly elected. No one shall be eligible to the office of President, Vice President, Secretary or Treasurer who is not a Trustee of the corporation.

Section 2: The President shall preside at all meetings of the Trustees and of the corporation, shall sign all written contracts for the corporation, and shall perform all such duties of his office. In his absence or disability the President's duties shall be performed by the Vice President.

Section 3: The Secretary shall issue notices of all Trustees and corporate meetings and shall attend and keep the minutes of the same, shall have charge of all corporate books, records and papers, shall be custodian of the corporate seal, shall attest with his signature and impress with the corporate seal all written contracts of the corporation, and shall perform all other duties as are incident to his office.

Section 4: The Treasurer shall have custody of all money and securities of the corporation and shall give bond in such sum as the Trustees may require. He shall sign all checks of the corporation and shall make a report of the general financial condition of the corporation at each annual meeting of the corporation.

ARTICLE VI

Section 1: The purposes for which this corporation is formed are to establish, maintain and promulgate a congregation of a church for Christian work and Christian activity and for the promotion of Christianity, and to maintain, ac-

- 2 -

quire, construct, remodel and refurbish property, real and personal, as may be necessary for carrying out the general purposes above declared; and to sell property both real and personal, tangible and intangible, and to borrow money and pledge the property of the corporation to secure the repayment thereof; and to do all legal and spiritual acts in order to promote or accomplish the purposes for which the said corporation is organized.

ARTICLE VII

Section 1:   The By-Laws of this corporation shall always be subordinate to the Constitution of the United States and Statutes of the State of Oklahoma, and more importantly, to the Holy Scriptures.

ARTICLE VIII

Section 1:   Amendments to these By-Laws may be made by a vote of the majority of the members present at any annual meeting consisting of a quorum of the Trustees, or at any special meeting thereof, when the proposed amendment has been set out in a notice of such meeting.

Now, therefore, be it resolved by the Board of Trustees that the By-Laws have been approved and adopted by a unanimous vote of the duly elected members of this corporation.

_____
President

_____
Vice President

_____
Secretary

First Day of Worship

At the last minute, Bob (Smokey) Stover was able to secure a place of worship for us. We were beginning to think we would have to worship in one of our homes, which we were prepared to do. We worshiped at the Broken Arrow Senior Citizens Center, South Main, Broken Arrow. from September 1, 2002 until June 6, 2004. We met for Bible study and worship, and evening worship on Sunday and for Wednesday night Bible Study. Each Sunday Craig Wooten put the sign out front, saying, "the Church of Christ at Whispering Hills meets here."

Senior Citizens Building, South Main

We had around 55 members when we began September 1, 2002, but a total of 106 people were present for our beginning; most were from the Broken Arrow congregation. That number began increasing every week. Sundays and Wednesdays found our members arriving early to perform various tasks necessary for Worship and Bible Study: preparing emblems for the Lord's Supper, setting up chairs and portable P.A. System, distributing song books. (The children especially enjoyed helping with this.) One of our members, Craig Wooten, put out the sign each Sunday which let the community know the "Church of Christ meets here."

Church of Christ at Whispering Hills, September 1, 2002

Fellowship continues to be a vital part of Whispering Hills!

First Fellowship

Even though it was necessary for some of us to come early to set up chairs and put out song books, and to reverse this process after each time we met, it was such a joy; we all worked together to do whatever needed to be done. Although current classroom space was limited, our teachers made do with portable classrooms. They brought all their supplies each week, and some even met in a hallway. One of our members, used her home computer to print bulletins, flyers, prayer lists, and pictorial directories. When we first moved to our new building, members volunteered to clean the building. When a task was needed, there was always someone stepping up to do it.

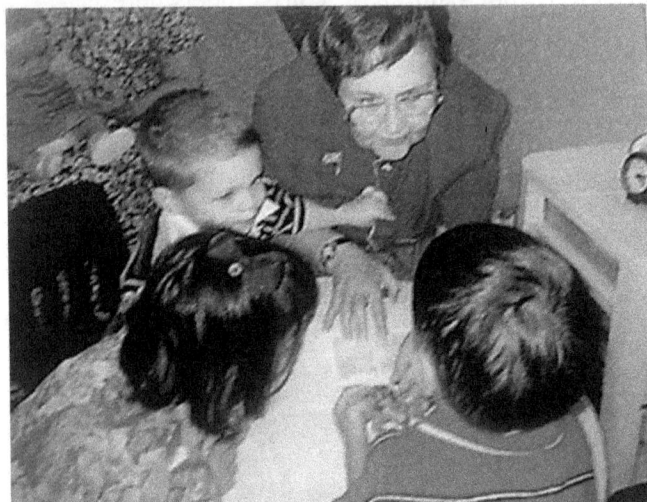

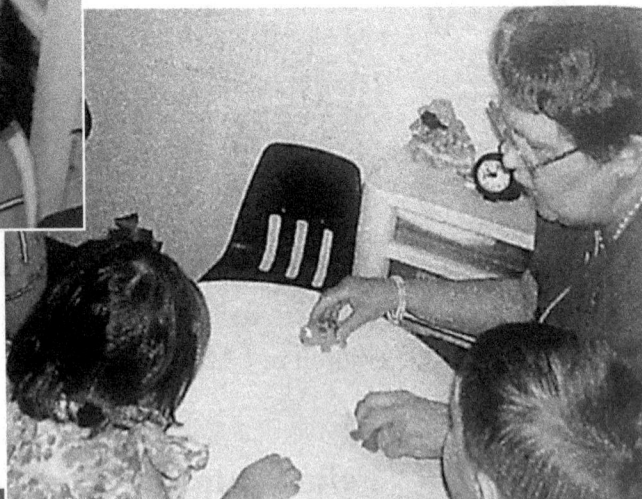

Winnie Matthews' Class in Hallway

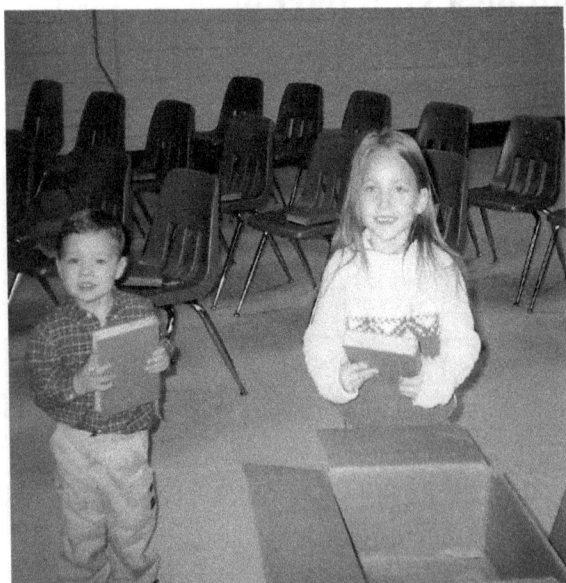

Evan Jowers, Wootens' Grandson, &
August Rain Matthews putting
Out Song Books.

**Charles Parette Preparing
Communion**

The men of the congregation unanimously approved using our own members and other local brethren to preach. This helped us utilize our resources to enable us to make the move to the church property as soon as possible. Kelly Riggs preached the first sermon for Whispering Hills on September 1, 2002, followed by Herschel Dyer on September 8.

Other local men who preached for us were: Charles Babb, Leon Brashears, Dave Brockway, Bill Burton, Terry Chaney, Donald Cherry, Justin Cherry, Clint Davidson, Bill Detherage, Rich Dolan, Bob Dreiling, Sidney Ellis, Lucian Farrar, Mark Farrar, Casey Flint, Jesse Gutierres, John Higgins, Jack Hill, Ralph Hunter, Brent Hutchins, Gary Jones, Dan Langdon (Try out), Bill Keele, Lee Keele, Scott Keele, Riley Killam, Charlie Kymes, Allen Lay, Robert Leitz, Brent Lightsey, Tony Lightsey, Harry Matthews (Glen's Brother), Kelly McCoy, Judge Morris, David Nielson, Jim Pinkston, Harry Riggs, Jr., David Rodriquez, Ray Rose, Steve Schinnerer, Mike Schrader, Dan Schnell, Denny Sneed, Mike Snider, Guy Suffridge, Lee Turner, Keith Walvoord, Billy Wilson, Cory Wilson, and others. FYI, the first speaker who actually spoke on the property was Riley Killam, grandson of Charles and Rae Parette. He gave us a lesson on a Wednesday night in June or July 2003.

Riley Killam

Elders Appointed

Most of the members of the new congregation had worshipped together at Broken Arrow for many years and knew each other well. It was the consensus of the newly formed congregation that we needed to have Elders installed as soon as possible in order to prevent future problems. The following men were appointed Elders October 6, 2002: Nathan Bell, Jerry Spradley, and Geames Wooten.

Jerry Spradley, Geames Wooten, Nathan Bell

Getting to
Know Our Elders

Nathan Bell

Nathan Bell grew up on a farm between Green Top and Queen City, MO. The nearest church was 25 miles away in Kirksville. His only sibling, a sister, still worships at Kirksville. She converted her husband before they married and he served as one of the Elders.

As Nathan's father and siblings were abandoned by their parents, members of the Church of Christ in Martinstown, MO took these children in and raised them. Nathan received his spiritual heritage from his "foster" grandparents, Orval & Mary Trammel; and because his grandmother loved his middle name "Nathan" so well, he changed his name from Lavern to Nathan to honor her memory. Nathan's foster grandparents taught Nathan's father and mother the truth. Nathan's father served as an Elder in the church for many years.

In High School, sports played an important part in his life as he played baseball, basketball, and ran track. He was Student Council President and also president of his Junior class. He attended York College in Nebraska for 2 years and played baseball while there. After finishing the two-year program at York College, he transferred to Oklahoma Christian College, now University. Instead of playing ball for them, he met and married Pam Bell. Pam's roommate at OCC was Nathan's sister. They met in September and were engaged after 6 weeks of courtship. They were married the following April.

Jennifer was born May 2 three years later and in August, this young family moved to Stigler, OK. While there he taught school and coached basketball, football, and track. Ralph Hunter was the minister at Stigler and this began a lifelong family friendship.

Heather and Matt were both born at St. Francis Hospital in Tulsa. Heather has just graduated from Oklahoma Christian and will be attending graduate school at OU beginning in August. Matt will be a Junior at Oklahoma Christian in August. Jennifer and husband, Davie, plan to go to Ireland in January 2005 after Davie receives his degree from Oklahoma Christian in December 2004.

Besides teaching school, Nathan has worked in the hardware business, sold toys to large businesses; and since 1983, has worked in a school fundraising business.
Nathan was a deacon in the Broken Arrow congregation, serving two different times. Nathan and Pam were a part of the Take-a-City Group #8, which was formed at the Broken Arrow congregation in January 2002. Nathan was installed as one of our elders at Whispering Hills in October 2002. We are indeed fortunate to have Nathan as one of our Elders at Whispering Hills and Pam as one of our Elder's wives. Nathan served from October 6, 2002 to August 2008. They now live in Houston, TX

- From bulletin dated August 3, 2003

Jerry Spradley

Jerry Spradley was born in Limestone, AR, October 28, 1946, to Ira and Ruby Adams Spradley. His mother was a member of the Church of Christ. His mother died in 1987, and his father passed away a few years ago. Jerry has a sister and brother older than he and two brothers younger. They were all born at home for a cost of $25 each.

Jerry graduated from high school at Deer, Arkansas in May of 1964, and has 60+ hours of college in Business Management and Human Recourse Management. His employment history consists of work at Sears Roebuck & Company in Missouri, General Motors Corp. in Kansas, U. S. Steel subsidary in Los Angeles, CA., and Public Service Company of Oklahoma. He officially retired from PSO in July of 2003 after 34 years of service.

Jerry returned to Arkansas from California for a month's vacation and started dating Diana. They had known each other in school. He asked Diana to marry him after dating only a few weeks. (Diana says after only one week, but surely not!) They were married on April 01, 1968. They have two children and a son-in-law, who were baptized at the Broken Arrow congregation. They also have two grandchildren, Jacob and Jessica, ages 9 & 7.

Diana was raised as a Baptist. Jerry believed in God, but didn't worship at any particular place. One Sunday afternoon his cousin, Johnny Giles, a member of the Broken Arrow congregation, invited him to go to church with him. Jerry promised he would visit church with him on Wednesday night if he would promise to leave him alone. That next Tuesday morning, Johnny was electrocuted at work. To keep his promise to him, Jerry visited the following Sunday and has never stopped going.

Jerry and Diana studied the Jule L. Miller film strips with James Haddock, the minister at the Bixby Church of Christ. Diana was baptized at the Bixby church in November of 1977. Jerry was baptized by Lee Peters on January 15, 1978, at the Broken Arrow Church of Christ. They placed membership at the Broken Arrow church in January of 1978, and worshiped there until moving to Whispering Hills September 1, 2002.

While at the Broken Arrow congregation, Jerry served as Deacon over the Building and Grounds Ministry for over 10 years. He taught 6th Grade boys and girls on Sunday mornings and 5th Grade boys on Wednesday nights. He also served as Deacon and Co-chairman of the Worship Ministry. He worked in the Communications Ministry for many years, and Diana worked with the young children for almost 20 years. Their final [last] ministry work was with the World Bible School with Russell and Margaret Teakell. Russell was the Ministry Chairman. This was their favorite work at the Broken Arrow congregation. It was very spiritually rewarding and they look forward to doing it again.

Jerry says, "Our greatest and most rewarding work has been the last 14 months working with the church of Christ at Whispering Hills. We thank God everyday for the rewarding experience we are having at this congregation. My favorite hobby is working at the building project and working with the other members of the Building Committee. I hope the second phase starts soon." Jerry was appointed an Elder at Whispering Hills and faithfully served until he resigned in 2015 to take out of town work.

Added: Since this was first written, Jerry's father became a Christian and has since passed away.

- From bulletin dated January 18, 2004

Geames Wooten

Geames was born August 2, 1935, in Fort Smith, AR to Clifford and Gladys Rae Craig Wooten. His mother died when he was 14 months old. Geames' mother, Gladys Rae Craig Wooten was not a Christian when she married, but was taught the truth by her mother-in-law, Amanda Lucinda Berry Wooten. The book "Eunice Lloyd" by R. L. Moody, a Gospel preacher, was also instrumental in her committing her life to Christ. This book was a fictional book telling the story of a girl searching for the truth. If you would like to read this book, talk to Lori.

Brother Moody held a Gospel meeting in Bloomer, AR and gave her the book to read; she was baptized and became a Christian. Strangely enough, this same book had an impact on Lori's life as her mother was reading that book before Lori was born. Lori (Eunice Lorine) was actually named for this book and her mother. Geames was raised by his father and step-mother, but the main spiritual influence for his life came from his grandparents, Rone and Lou Berry Wooten, of Mansfield, AR. He graduated from Lavaca, AR High School in 1954 and entered the Air Force, where he spent four years. Geames attended Tulsa Junior College and University of Tulsa. When Geames received his honorable discharge from the Air Force, he began working for the Census Bureau in Kansas. In 1961, Geames came to Tulsa to work for Minehoma Finance and began attending 10th & Rockford Church of Christ. Geames grew up in the church, but had never obeyed the Gospel. He knew the truth, and had determined that when he came to Tulsa he would become a Christian and look for a Christian wife.

Geames and Lori met at a Halloween party in October 1961, given by the Young Professionals at 10th Street Church of Christ. Geames had just come to town and all the girls were wondering who the new guy in town was with the red Austin-Healey. They were introduced at the party and had their first date the following Thursday night. The night prior to their first date, Geames was baptized into Christ by Herschel Dyer at 10th Street in Tulsa. Geames attended worship with Lori on Sunday nights at Springdale Church of Christ in Tulsa and was asked to lead a prayer. That first time he declined as he was not prepared; but by the next week he was. That was the beginning of his Christian service.

They dated steadily and on April 4th, the night before Lori's 21st birthday, Geames asked her to marry him and gave her a ring. They met in October 1961, and were married the following September 1. They lived in Tulsa and moved to Broken Arrow in September 1964; Craig was 4 months old. Tracy came along in 1967.

Geames and Lori both taught Bible classes at the Broken Arrow Church. Geames became a Deacon in the late sixties and served until being appointed as an Elder in 1982. He served as an Elder until August 2002, a month before the church at Whispering Hills began. They have worked in campaigns in Broken Arrow, Cameron, MO, Tver, Russia, Avdeevka, Ukraine, Poland and visited the Florence Bible School in Florence, Italy, which Broken Arrow supported for many years. Mission work was an important part in their lives and still is.

Geames became an Elder of the church of Christ at Whispering Hills on October 6, 2002, and for seven months became part of the construction team, along with a few other men of our congregation. He just thought he was retired!

The family enjoyed camping and a highlight on their trips was worshipping with Christians all over the United States and abroad. Geames and Lori looked forward to many rewarding years working in the Kingdom alongside their brothers and sisters at Whispering Hills. One of Geames' favorite verses in the Bible is Isaiah 26:3 - *You will keep in perfect peace him whose mind is steadfast, because he trusts in you.* NIV.

Added: Geames and Lori also taught Bible classes at Whispering Hills; Lori did the bulletin each week and the pictorial directory as needed. Geames served the church at Whispering Hills faithfully as one of the Elders from October 6, 2002 until his death February 27, 2011.

- From bulletin dated February 19, 2004

Planning for the New Facility

A planning session was held at the Wootens and plans were beginning to take shape. The men made lists of things to be accomplished prior to construction. First of all, they had to have a perk test done, building site graded and leveled and utilities decided on.

Putmans, Aitkenhead, Parettes, Wootens, Spradley, Matthews, Wadsworths

In order to save as much as possible on construction costs, a building committee was formed and acted as the contractor, with Russell Wadsworth being in charge. He later resigned and Walter Sorrell became the new person in charge. Les Brewer, a construction builder, now deceased, who was a member of the Broken Arrow congregation, also helped oversee the construction of the building.

Pre-Construction

Charles Parette, Jeremy & Russell Wadsworth, Everett Putman, Geames Wooten, and Glen Matthews looking for best place for a perk test.

Geames Wooten spreading dirt and gravel for construction site.

Groundbreaking

Elders' Interview with the Ledger, 1-3-03

Twenty years ago, the Elders of the Broken Arrow Church of Christ planned and dreamed of establishing another congregation of the Lord's people in Broken Arrow. Approximately two years ago, 20 acres of land was donated in South Broken Arrow for the purpose of establishing another congregation. A Take-a-City Group was established at the Broken Arrow Church of Christ in January 2002 and a core group was formed from that group.

Since January 2002, Take-a-City Group 8, composed of several families of the Broken Arrow Church of Christ, has been working toward further evangelizing the Broken Arrow community and the surrounding area through the avenue of this new congregation in South Broken Arrow. Some of the members of the TAC Group 8 committed themselves to become charter members of the Church of Christ at Whispering Hills. Others in the TAC Group 8 remain members of the Broken Arrow Church of Christ and will continue to support the new congregation until such time as it is able to stand alone.

The new congregation of the Lord's church was established on Sunday, the first day of September 2002, and the following Elders were ordained October 6, 2002, according to the pattern found in the New Testament: Nathan Bell, Jerry Spradley, and Geames Wooten.

The Church of Christ at Whispering Hills will be located at 21349 East 111th Street, Broken Arrow. Our temporary meeting place is The Main Place, 1800 South Main, Broken Arrow. We invite you to come worship with us. Schedule of our services is as follows:

Sunday: Bible Class - 9:00 a.m. - Worship 10:00 a.m. & 6:00 p.m.
Wednesday Ladies Bible Class - 9:00 a.m.
Wednesday Evening Class & Devotional - 7:00 p.m.

We ask for the continued prayers of the Broken Arrow congregation and others as we establish this work. We seek the continued encouragement and support of Take-A-City Group 8. Without the mission minded efforts of the eldership of the Broken Arrow Church, this new work would be only a dream.

Being a part of the Broken Arrow Church of Christ has blessed our lives and brought about the missionary spirit that is so prevalent in the church at Whispering Hills. It is this missionary spirit that will help make the new work a real glory to God in our community. Our groundbreaking ceremony was held Sunday, January 5 at 2:00 p.m.

Deed Presented to Whispering Hills

The Broken Arrow Eldership was satisfied that the Whispering Hills congregation was a Bible based, doctrinally sound body of the Lord's people. On December 12, 2002, Broken Arrow deeded the 20 acres to the Church of Christ at Whispering Hills and presented the deed to the Whispering Hills Elders January 6, 2003.

Gerry Lynn, Elder, Broken Arrow Church of Christ presenting
deed to Jerry Spradley, Geames Wooten, Nathan Bell, Elders of
Church of Christ at Whispering Hills

Groundbreaking, Cont'd

God has blessed us with the land and the growth. Now it's time to build a building! We need the support of other Christians to do this, and we ask you to prayerfully consider helping with this work.

Literally Breaking Ground

Note from Bill Keele

(From May 18, 2003 Bulletin)

I had the opportunity to speak at Whispering Hills Sunday, May 11, 2003. They are doing well. They are making plans to start building on the property we deeded to them as soon as possible. I know they had wanted to start earlier, but "hitches" are common in trying to get things like that off the ground. I get reports of the evangelistic work that they are doing and are excited about. They have ordained three elders – Nathan Bell, Jerry Spradley, and Geames Wooten. They are continuing to use guest speakers in an effort to save money for the building project. A number of Broken Arrow men have been among those guest speakers.

God is blessing our area with another fine congregation at Whispering Hills. We join other great churches in helping give birth to a new congregation. The church throughout the centuries has grown as one church plants another. God bless Whispering Hills. God bless the Broken Arrow congregation, too.

- Bill Keele, Minister
Broken Arrow Church of Christ

The gas line was already on 111th, but water had to be brought across the street. Rod Copelin and crew took care of bringing the water line under the 211th and onto the property. Several men of the congregation helped.

Robert Brown

God never saves a spectator

I have no right to work out my own salvation in the way I choose.

Helen Roseveare

Deacons Appointed

In June 2003, eight deacons were appointed to serve the new congregation at Whispering Hills. They were: Eddie Bates, Lawrence Buckner, David Foster, Everett Putman, Ed Rentie, Walter Sorrell, Bob Stover, and Russell Teakell.

Eddie Bates
Ed Rentie

Lawrence Buckner
Walter Sorrell

David Foster
Bob Stover

Everett Putman
Russell Teakell

We have been blessed with continued growth through baptisms, restorations, and those who have placed membership. Jesus taught "By this all men will know you are my disciples, if you have love one for another." (John 13:35) Come visit and you will find friendly, warmhearted, evangelistic Christians.

First Minister Selected

Dan and Kathy Langdon had been missionaries first in Japan for two years, and then in Scotland for six years. In January 1999, they moved to Glenrothes, Scotland and were there six years. In March of 2004, the Langdons came to the states to find a position at home. Dan preached in several places, but almost as soon as he preached at the Church of Christ at Whispering Hills, the elders knew they had found their minister.

They desired to move back to the states to be closer to their aging parents. On April 4, 2004, Dan and Kathy Langdon along with their four children Liem, Abby, Levi, and Anna Grace came to Whispering Hills while we were meeting in the Senior Citizens Center. Dan preached both lessons. The Wootens had a fellowship for the Langdons Sunday night after evening worship and everyone loved them. The Elders had not planned to hire a minister that soon, but decided after much prayer and planning that they would go ahead and hire Dan, as they felt they would attract young families., which they certainly did.

The Langdons were with us for our first day of worship on June 6, 2004 in our new building. They found a house while they were in Broken Arrow and would close on it when the moved from Scotland in August. We continued growing.

Langdon First Minister of Whispering Hills

By Lucienda Denson, Lifestyle Editor of Broken Arrow Ledger

Dan Langdon and his family have come home. "He is our pulpit minister, our preacher," said Geames Wooten, an elder with Church of Christ at Whispering Hills.

The family of six took a meandering route from Oklahoma City to Broken Arrow that included long "lay overs" in Japan and Scotland over a period of ten years.

Dan was born in Pennsylvania and grew up in New Jersey. He went to Northeastern Christian Junior College and transferred to Oklahoma Christian University in Oklahoma City. He and his wife, Kathy met at Oklahoma Christian. They have four children: Liam 7, Abby 5, Levi 4, and Anna Grace 2.

When the Langdons finished college, they accepted an opportunity to live in Japan and teach High School English as a second language. The project sponsored by the Japanese government and overseen by an American, allowed them to teach using the Biblc.

They also worked for the Mito Church of Christ and the Hitachi-tago Church of Christ. From that experience, they knew they wanted to be in a full-time ministry. Dan is an English teacher by education, but their passion for mission work and sharing the Gospel happened in Japan. The Langdons began looking for a place where they could live and work in a ministry. They had been on a mission campaign in Scotland in 1993 so that seemed an appropriate place to begin. They followed up on some of those contacts and ended up forming a team with Russell and Jennifer Hill. They moved to Dundee, Scotland, in December 1996 and worked for two years at the Dundee Church of Christ.

Open House

RELIGION   **BROKEN ARROW DAILY LEDGER**   **Thursday October 14, 2004**
PAGE 5

Just under two years from the ground breaking ceremony for the Church of Christ at Whispering Hills, the congregation will hold an open house in its new building.

We will have an Open House at 2 p.m. Sunday. We're inviting all our friends, family, building contractors and all the churches in the area to come be with us for this event," said Geames Wooten, one of the church's elders. Other elders are Nathan Bell and Jerry Spradley. The structure is the first phase of a master plan that began more than twenty years ago at the Broken Arrow Church of Christ. As Broken Arrow continued to expand to the southeast, the congregation began to consider a second congregation to accommodate those residents.

Several families from the Broken Arrow Church of Christ committed themselves to becoming members of a new congregation to meet that need, the Church of Christ at Whispering Hills. The groundbreaking took place on Sunday, January 5, 2003, on the 20 acres donated for the church. While the church building was being constructed, it wasn't unusual to see Scout and Christian Youth Groups camping on the property. That's precisely what both congregations had in mind from the beginning.

Our dream is to use every inch of the 20 acres for Christian Service. We already have a beautiful outdoor amphitheater built by the Eagle Scouts sponsored from the Broken Arrow congregation that local Christian Scout groups, and other organizations use. We foresee so much more to come — ball fields, camping areas, a retreat center, and more. God has given to us so we can give back in His name. Our prayer is that people will see God in all that we do, and find God in what we can share. The church building is located at 21349 E 111th Street S near the NSU-Broken Arrow campus. Bible study will be at 9 a.m., Worship at 10 a.m., and our Open House at 2 p.m. The Church of Christ at Whispering Hills has already held services in the building, which will be the focus of an Open House at 2 p.m. Sunday. The new Minister, Dan Langdon, and wife Kathy, along with their four children have moved to Broken Arrow from Scotland.

Church of Christ at Whispering Hills

Broken Arrow, Oklahoma

Section Two

Ministries

Ministry Outline

Attendance	Charles Bower
Benevolence	Allen Messick
Building and Grounds	E. J. Smith
Education/Youth	Daniel Hodges
LTC	Steve Parrott
Finance	Steve Parrott
Missions	The Elders
Bible Call (discontinued)	
Cambodia	
India	
Italy	
Philippines	
Ukraine	
World Bible School	Jan Laney
World English Institute	Lori Wooten, Dewey Johnson, Shaun Collins
Individual Mission Efforts	
Security	Kenneth Houston
Visitation	Joe Kelley
Women's	
Clothing Exchange	Rebecca LeDoux, Kara Snider
Scheduling as Needs Arise	Faye Ellis, Rae Parette, Lori Wooten
Sewing Group	Lyuba Teakell
Worship	E. J. Smith, Carlton Pittman
Zone Groups	Dale Graham

Benevolence

The Church of Christ at Whispering Hills is a very caring and benevolent congregation and practices benevolence in numerous ways, especially by meeting special needs of our congregation and those outside. We have Zone groups that provide meals when needed. We also have numerous people who provide transportation to and from medical facilities and who also take care of particular needs that may arise.

Some of the outside needs we have contributed to are:

Hurricane Rita in 2005 - Church at Winnie, Texas, where M. A. Hendrickson, Martha Parrott's father, is the minister. Their building was seriously damaged and we contributed to help restore their building.

Hurricane Katrina Relief - On September 4, 2005, the entire contribution from previous week and portion of this week's contribution was sent to White's Ferry Road Church of Christ for Katrina Hurricane Victims. We helped the Broken Arrow congregation sort clothes and other items to be sent. We also helped the Coweta congregation pay for fuel to take two semis to Gulf Port, MS. Jerry Spradley and former member, Gene Dunham, drove a semi to the New Orleans area and were escorted to the particular area by the police.

Participated in Angel Tree in December 2005 and 2006. The daughter of Virgil and Genelle Harris worked at the OU-Tulsa IMPACT Team. This team of doctors, nurses, and therapists provide services to over 55 adults who suffer from severe mental illness. Most have no family who will associate with them. They live on the street or in bare, cheap apartments. They have their own unique stories and have made lists of items they want for Christmas. We participated in this program a couple of years. One year, we had them come to WH for their Christmas party and the next year the Harrises and Wootens delivered gifts to them at the OU-Tulsa IMPACT Team.

Hurricane Harvey - On September 17, 2017 a special contribution for victims in Houston, TX area was made.

We have also helped members of the church in the Philippines where our member, Joe Kelley,
participates in an annual mission trip.

Youth Education

Since the beginning of the Whispering Hills congregation, the children who have attended Whispering Hills have been blessed with a wonderful youth education department that includes structured Bible classes, fellowship opportunities, and involvement in Bible-based programs outside of the congregation such as LTC, Preachers/Teachers Camp, and summer church camp.

Sunday morning and Wednesday evening Bible classes in the Infants through 6th Grade focus on quarterly arranged lessons from the Old and New Testaments. Many dedicated members of the congregation have worked to teach and organize these classes. A few years ago, a Sunday evening worship training class was begun for children 3 years old through 4th grade. The 7th-12th grade Bible classes, often called the Teen Class, have been taught by many members of the congregation and seek to further the knowledge and understanding of the Bible gained in earlier years in the elementary wing. Girls and Boys classes are often offered separately and on occasion meet together for bigger group discussions of Bible topics that are of particular concern to their age group. The current minister, Dale Graham, as well as the current elders, have all taught the Teen classes and have been active in helping the youth program.

Over the years, many of the youth have attended church camp at both Quartz Mountain Christian Camp and Burnt Cabin Christian Camp. Several young men have attended the Future Preachers Camp while several young ladies have also attended. Many types of fellowship opportunities have been organized for the youth including regular Teen Devos, group outings to local activities, service projects for members of the congregation, lock-ins, etc.

- Daniel Hodges

A separate girls' class for those in 7th through 12th grade has for the last several years been taught by Martha Parrott with helpers Elizabeth and Lyuba Teakell, and Lori Wooten. Elders' wives and other ladies of the church have also taught.

A separate boys' class has also been held for those 7th through 12th grade, with Daniel Hodges being the main teacher, with the Elders and Minister also teaching from time to time. At the present time these two classes are combined.

Bible Classes
Pre School - 6th Grade

Teachers: Winnie Matthews, Margaret Teakell,
Students: Kayci Snider, Sarah Bates, Nick Dreiling, Aaron
Mitchell, Kayelynn Chase

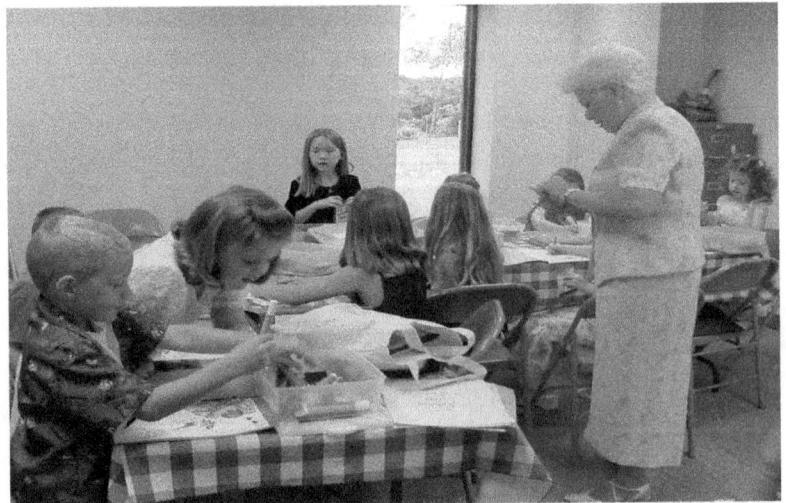

Grayson Snider, Sarah Bates, August Rain Matthews
Barbara Buckner, Teacher

Pre School - 6th Grade, Cont'd

Kristi Chandlers's 2 & 3 Year Old Bible Class

JoAnn Graham's 4 & 5 Year Old Bible Class

Lisa Putman's 1st - 3rd Grade Bible Class

Doris Pittman's 4th - 6th Grade Bible Class

Teen Combined Bible Class

College & Young Adult

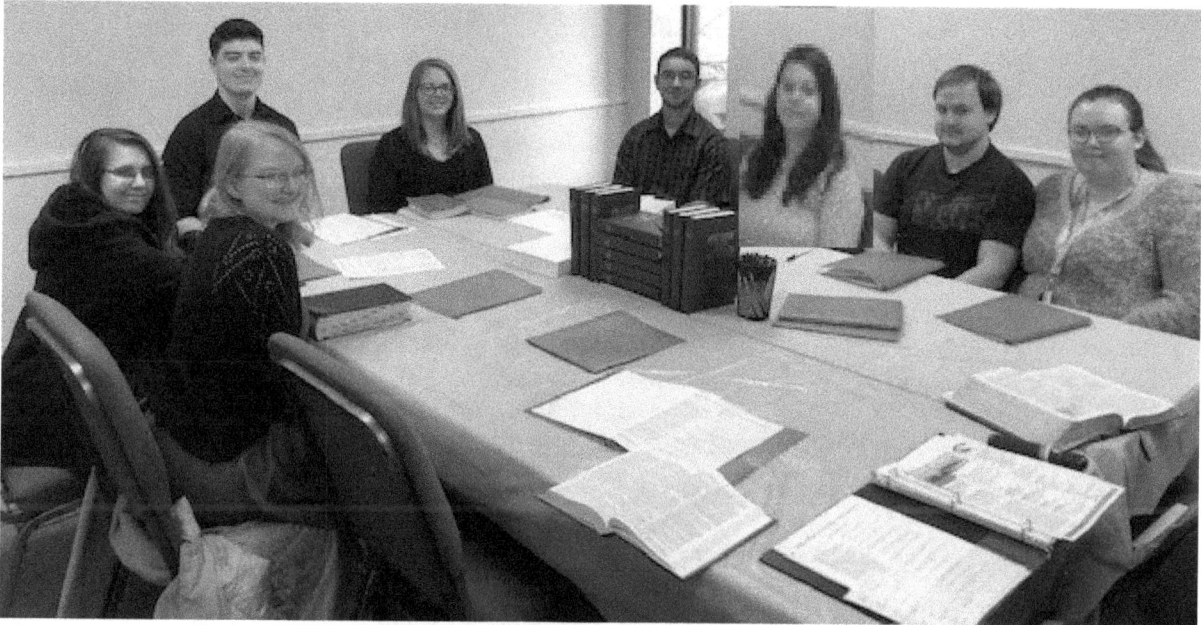

Makayla Dreiling, Hannah Collins, Justin Chandler, Taylor Lee,
Josh VanTuyl, Sarah Bates, Aaron & Katie Collins

Adult Bible Class 2002

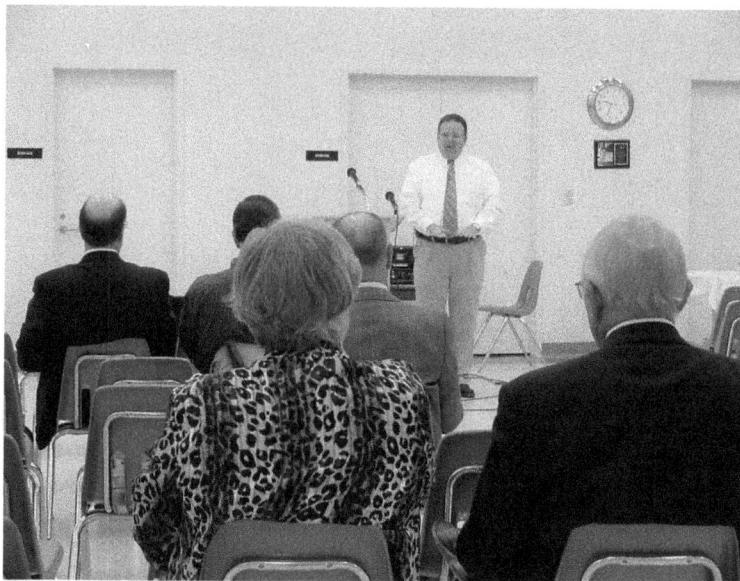

Nathan Bell, Teacher

Dale Graham's Class - Fellowship Hall

Auditorium Class

Ladies Bible Class

An announcement from our bulletin of September 8, 2002:

> Ladies Bible Class Wednesday, 9:30 a.m. in the home of Rae Parette, 7423 S. Gafford Blvd., BA. Winnie Matthews will begin teaching in Genesis. Answer this question for class homework. How long was Noah and his family in the ark?

Our Ladies Bible Class continued meeting weekly in each others homes until sometime in 2006. We developed very close ties. We met a few times in the building, but was soon discontinued. A short time later we began meeting once a month in each other's homes as it was more inviting.

Picture 1 - Margaret Campbell's Home
Picture 2 - Louise Adam's Home
Picture 3 - Lori Wooten's Home

For the last few years, we have met once a month in the home of Marcia Lightsey, a wife of one of our Elders. Marcia always begins with a devotion and then one of the ladies takes turns doing a spiritual lesson applicable to our lives. We then have food and fellowship with everyone bringing a finger food, etc. Come join us for a most special evening the second Tuesday of the month. Recently, other ladies have volunteered their homes as Marcia is recovering from surgery.

Our ladies

to study

God's Word!

Ladies Day
April 30, 2005

Take Time
To Be Holy

Church of Christ
At Whispering Hills
Broken Arrow, Oklahoma

Registration
and
Breakfast
0900-0930

Welcome
Lori Wooten

Opening Prayer
Rae Parette

Singing
Kathy Langdon

Scripture Reading
Martha Rentie

Introduction of Speaker
Pam Bell

Lesson I
"The Beauty of Holiness"

Singing

Prayer
Betty Boggs

Lunch

Congregation Recognition
Lori Wooten

Singing

Scripture Reading
Susie McDrummond

Lesson II
"You Are Standing On Holy Ground"

Dismissal Comments
Pam Bell

Dismissal Prayer
Cindy Sampson

Ladies Day, Cont'd

Ladies
Day
Cont'd

Missions Ministry

Bible Call

We had the Bible Call program for a few years, but when the machine had problems, we did not continue it. It is a very helpful biblical tool with scriptures. There is also a notebook in our Library with all the subjects which you can copy; be sure to put the original back in the notebook.

Bible Call is a free public service religious information library consisting of hundreds of five-minute recorded messages on a wide variety of Bible Subjects. The material was carefully researched and written by over one hundred prominent religious leaders from across the nation. The BIBLE CALL library makes it possible for anyone wishing to study the Bible to locate information on almost any important topic quickly and accurately.

Even though we no longer have the program at Whispering Hills, you can access the program by dialing the following number:

(931) 473-CALL (2255)

BIBLE CALL TELEPHONE LIBRARY

Hear **Free** Recorded Information On **Hundreds Of Bible Subjects including:**

SELF-IMPROVEMENT
PERSONAL
SALVATION
FAMILY LIFE
BIBLE STUDY
WORSHIP
THE CHURCH
ETERNITY
SCIENCE & RELIGION
CHRISTIAN EVIDENCES
ESPECIALLY FOR TEENAGERS
ESPECIALLY FOR CHILDREN
MORALITY
GENERAL INTEREST

The material was carefully researched and written by over one hundred prominent religious leaders from across the nation

The Bible Call Library makes it possible for anyone wishing to study the Bible to locate information on almost any important topic quickly and accurately.

Since Bible Call is now completely automated, it is available twenty-four hours a day, seven days a week. Just call the number listed above from any Touch-Tone phone and follow the instructions given.

Select the subjects you would like to hear from the list and request each topic by its number.

What Else?

"Why ask me what is good?" Jesus replied. "Only God is good. But to answer your question, you can receive eternal life if you keep the commandments." "Which ones?" the man asked. And Jesus replied: "Do not murder. Do not commit adultery. Do not steal. Do not testify falsely. Honor your father and mother. Love your neighbor as yourself." "I've obeyed all these commandments," the young man replied. "What else must I do?" (Matthew 19:17-20)

Key Thought: Wow, can you believe somebody actually had the audacity to say it? "I've obeyed all these, so what's next for me to check off my list so I can go to heaven?" We sometimes think a checklist might be nice so that we could check off the items we need to do to ensure our entry into heaven. Thankfully, God didn't give us one. The Old Testament Law was a list of commands and demands God gave, but no one could fulfill it. All fell short. Even worse, many tried to judge themselves by comparing themselves with others to see how many more things on the list they could check off than the other person. Most sad of all, in the process of checking lists and comparing righteousness, many forgot to give their hearts to God. They made something beautiful and precious into religious formality and façade. The young man in this story falls into this last category. He was not a bad person. In fact, compared to most in his day he was probably most exemplary. But his list left little room for giving himself, and what he held most dear, to the Lord. It was the one "thing" he lacked, and it was everything, because he had not yielded his heart.

- Selected

Cambodia Bible Institute

Since August 2007, Rich and Ronda Dolan have been working in Phnom Penh, Cambodia, teaching men and women about God's plan of salvation through Jesus, and equipping them to teach others. Rich Dolan is the director of CBI, which is under the umbrella of Sunset International Bible Institute. Sunset has 50 Associate Schools throughout the world.

They have overseen the graduation of 42 students from the Cambodia Bible Institute, 31 of whom received a Bachelor's Degree from the Sunset School of Preaching. Their students have gone on to plant churches and teach their families about the Good News. In 2007, a city of 3-4 million had only two congregations. There are now six for certain, and many other students have returned to their homes in rural areas to be lights in their communities. In total, over 23 new congregations have been planted in the country as the result of CBI students' efforts.

In addition to teaching students year round, Rich and Ronda oversee the translation of Bible study books from English to Khmer. Books like "Historical Christian Evidences" by Ed Wharton and "Life of Christ" by Richard Rogers reinforce and further explain the truth that students read in the Bible. This is a thriving and growing effort to give the people of Cambodia every chance to be affected by the Truth. Many denominational leaders use these books, giving even more people the chance to read Acts and Romans from a proper perspective for the first time.

They have overseen the graduation of 42 students from the Cambodia Bible Institute, 31 of whom received a Bachelor's Degree from the Sunset School of Preaching. Their students have gone on to plant churches and teach their families about the Good News. In 2007, a city of 3-4 million had only two congregations. There are now six for certain, and many other students have returned to their homes in rural areas to be lights in their communities. In total, over 23 new congregations have been planted in the country as the result of CBI students' efforts.

In addition to teaching students year round, Rich and Ronda oversee the translation of Bible study books from English to Khmer. Books like "Historical Christian Evidences" by Ed Wharton and "Life of Christ" by Richard Rogers reinforce and further explain the truth that students read in the Bible. This is a thriving and growing effort to give the people of Cambodia every chance to be affected by the Truth. Many denominational leaders use these books, giving even more people the chance to read Acts and Romans from a proper perspective for the first time.

India

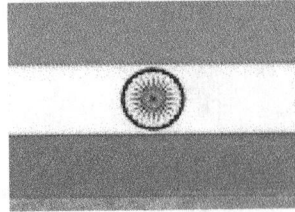

We began supporting the orphanage Brother A. Visweswara Rao began in Arikirevula, India shortly after Whispering Hills began. His ministry includes preaching for two congregations and a Leper Colony, oversight of an orphanage and a widows program, Preachers Training School, TV Program, etc.

The work of the church in India began several years ago when a Canadian minister accompanied by Bill Paxton made a trip to India. In one of the gospel meetings, the father of Brother A. Visweswara Rao (Brother V) and Brother V as well was baptized into Christ and the father began the church in Arikirevula.

Brother V was just a child when his father became a Christian. His father was a day laborer, the lowest caste in India, and also preached for the church. In India, the caste system is still very much in place and it's impossible to rise to a higher caste. Even though Brother V had a banking degree, he could never find a job in banking because he was from the lowest caste. Brother V then went to a Bible Training School in India where he received a degree or certificate. When his father passed away, Brother V became the minister of the Church of Christ at Arikirevula.

Orphanage

Andre-Predisch is 30 km from coast, in a poor agricultural area. About 1998, a tsunami hit the coast of India when several parents were killed and a great need arose for an orphan's home in Arikirevula. Brother V was asked to minister to these orphans. Bill and Shirley Paxton were instrumental in raising money for the orphanage, which is registered with the government as the Christian Charitable Society. So the Bill and Shirley Paxton Children's Home came into existence. They can take care of as many as 75 children aged 6 – 18.

The Warden runs the day to day operation of the orphanage. He receives a salary of $75 a month. Whispering Hills helps with the work of the orphanage. The first floor of Brother V's former house is where the church meets. The girls' dorm is on the second floor, which is overseen by one of the two widows who works for the orphanage. The full time widows do the meals, cleaning, laundry, take care of the children, etc. They receive free room and board along with $5 a month. There is also an apartment on the third floor where visitors stay.

A building was built across the street from the church building and the girls' dorm to house the dining hall, kitchen and food preparation and storage area; the boys' dorm is on the top floor and the Warden supervises them. His apartment is in this building along with Brother V's mother. One of the former orphans who grew up in the home serves as Youth Director and plans activities for the youth. The High School students attend a public high school while Bro V pays a fee for the younger students to attend a better elementary school. The younger children walk to school which is nearby, but Bro V pays three drivers of three wheelers to transport High School students because of the great distance

Church of Christ at Kovvur

Brother V started another congregation in Kovvur, which is a short distance down the road from Arikirevula; they now have 100 members. He also continues to preach for the congregation at Arikirevula, first at Kovvur where he lives and later at Arikirevula. Brother V and Shekina first lived in a little shack and slept on the floor and when it rained, the roof leaked When the Paxtons found out their living conditions, a Dallas attorney gave $20,000 for them to build a house. Bro V had to make a loan for the rest but was able to build a nice home there. The church is on the first floor, with their apartment on the second. They also have a houseboy who helps Shekina clean; he is also Brother V's driver and right hand man who takes photos., etc.

Activities in which brother V is involved:

Preaches for two congregations – Arikirevula and Kovvur
Oversees Orphanage Students with help of the Warden who supervises.
Preaches for Leper Colony
Preacher Training School began 2017 – 3 days a week; 8 became gospel preachers, extensive follow up
TV Program – 2 baptized
Preaches gospel at denominational churches
Sewing Class for students
Preacher's Meeting once a month with 35 preachers in the area

- Info from Keith Walvoord 3.8.18

Italy

Jeremy Korodaj was a missionary in Italy that we supported for several year; our support was discontinued when he left.

Philippines

The Philippine work started in 1995 as Joe Kelley's own personal good work and support for Bro. Robert Gamaio in Tuguegaro City, Philippines.

It continued that way until 2005 when the elders of 10th and Rockford church of Christ started helping with Robert's support. Joe's first mission trip was in January of 2007. It was a two-week trip to personally meet Bro. Robert and to evaluate the work there. They were able to visit around 18 congregations and hold what several classes over a three-day period for 50 local ministers. He quickly learned our separation of some 9,000 miles limited what could be done to assist the brethren. It was decided, to first focus on the local ministers by providing lectureships and sound biblical material for their study and learning. By helping these ministers increase their biblical knowledge they would be better equipped to proclaim the gospel of Christ more accurately and guide the congregations that they are working with to be more scripturally correct in their service to the Lord.

Secondly, to visit as many of the local congregations in order to provide encouragement to be faithful and strong in the Lord, and third, to provide limited benevolence where possible, and to see and evaluate each congregation as to their scriptural needs and composition. This type of mission format has proven to be effective and beneficial for the past 10 years.

From 2007 to 2017, our efforts have been blessed with 384 new souls being brought to Christ and added to His Kingdom. I have visited over 40 different congregations in 4 different provinces in the northeast sector on the main island of Luzon. A few areas of misunderstanding have been addressed and corrected. It has not been my intention to "Americanize" them, but only to teach the gospel of Christ, to encourage, to uplift, and to provide limited assistance where I can. My mission trips would not be possible if it weren't for the support from seven faithful congregations and some soul-loving individuals. It is my goal and desire to continue this work as long as the Lord can use my efforts in this way. The gospel of Christ has been gladly received by many; they heard, they believed, and they obeyed. Our brothers and sisters in Christ in the Philippines are honest, hard-working individuals who love the Lord and His church and deserve our attention.

-Joe Kelley

Ukraine

The fall and early winter season of 2017 was an especially busy time for us in Ukraine. Kevin Hahn is the preacher of the Lake Houston congregation in Humble, TX.—our sponsoring church. It was a real delight having Kevin and his wife, Heather, spend a short but intensive time with us in our various fields of work. Kevin and Heather showed an intuitive understanding of how to relate to people of another culture and gave encouraging lessons to our Christians in Poltava, Zaporozhye, Kamianske and Verkhnedneprovsk.

Poltava is the base location of our work in Ukraine and Gary and Nadya have been a team in this work for the last ten years. The church in Poltava was established on December 1, 1994. From that time till now - 23 years later - it has been meeting in rented facilities in various locations. The facility in use right now is the best of all those that preceded it, but we have been literally running out of room. Nearly three years ago, a large section of the ground floor of a high-rise building went up for sale right in the very location where we have been renting. This is a 110 square meter facility that will be ideal for the Poltava church, and it is even ready for immediate occupancy. We can purchase this facility which is 110 square meters which is a large section of the ground floor of a high-rise building for $70,000 and have already raised more than $40,000. They feel very strongly that this facility not slip through their fingers, but the closing date is coming closer

The Lord's church in Kamianske is comprised of two congregations, which we refer to as the Left Bank and the Right Bank churches. The Left Bank meeting place was the center of a lot of activity in the fall. When the Hahns were present, we arranged a joint meeting of both groups and nearly overflowed the assembly room. We also had several special studies conducted in the Left Bank facility with excellent attendance every time. It is gratifying that we seem to be making a lot of headway in showing Christians how to be Bible-oriented in their lives and in their church meetings. We have also been conducting separate men's and women's meetings so as to focus on the particular needs of each group.

The church in Verkhnedneprovsk is what we might call a house-church, since it meets in a member's home. It is reminiscent of Paul's statement to the Romans to "greet Priscilla and Aquila" and the "the church tha is in their house." Thankfully, the sweet sister who hosts this meeting place is both gracious and untiring in providing for the needs of the saints. The church gathers here two days a week, without fail, and regardless of the weather.

63

World Bible School

World Bible School began at Whispering Hills when we moved to our new church building by Russell and Margaret Teakell. Jan Laney joined the Teakells and a few weeks later Louise Adams, Diana Spradley and Barbara Buckner joined them. Those currently working in WBS are: Barbara Buckner, Doris Pittman, Tara Ryan, Kara Snider, Diana Spradley and Jan Laney.

They send out nine lessons, mostly to Africa and England. When Carolyn Kusler joined them, she was given 15 names of prisoners who were in Texas prisons. Each of the ladies send lessons to foreign countries and to the prisoners.

They send out around 30 to 40 Bible lessons to prisoners in Texas and some to foreign countries. Since the first of the year, they have sent 8 names to their contact in Texas who have requested baptism. They are the following: Lovelady, Tx. Fredenico Villareal, Emilio Ballep, Randy Ray Tredway - Jimmy Hornsby, Rosharon, Tx., Shelby Kindrick, Tenn. Colony, Tx., Joseph Schiefelbein, Overton, Tx. We have not received word whether or not they were baptized. Hopefully they have been and are our new brothers in Christ.

- Jan Laney

World English Institute (WEI)

WEI is designed to attract students who are studying English as a second language and to teach them by using the Bible as an English textbook. While the students are learning English, they are also learning the Scriptures. Some seed falls in good and honest hearts and brings forth fruit (Luke 8:15). God gives the increase (I Corinthians 3:7)

Lori Wooten began working with WEI in 1999 after a mission trip to Ukraine in 1998, as she wanted to continue studying with Helena (pronounced Elaine) from Avdevka, who was baptized into Christ after her WEI studies. During the last few years she has had to leave her home because of the Russian-Separatists.

Deborah Houston joined WEI for a while instructing students, but had to quit because of circumstances. Shawn Collins and Dewey Johnson came on board as teachers after a WEI representative introduced the work to our congregation in 2017. Dewey has had 2 studies and one of those is about to complete all the lessons. It has been a most rewarding work as you become personally involved with people all over the world, and makes it possible to carry out the Great Commission while staying at home. Shaun has had 22 studies with four currently active. His particular area is Uganda.

Individual Mission Efforts

Chimala - Archer Honea 2017 and 2018

Sopot, Poland – Lori Wooten – October 2012

El Salvadore - Micah & Lisa Waldroop - June 2005

Ten Things God Won's Ask
On the Day You Die

1. God won't ask what kind of car you drove, He'll ask how many people you drove who didn't have transportation.

2. God won't ask the square footage of your house, He'll ask how many people you welcomed into your home.

3. God won't ask about the clothes you had in your closet, He'll ask how many you helped to clothe.

4. God won't ask what your highest salary was, He'll ask if you compromised your character to obtain it.

5. God won't ask what your job title was, He'll ask if you performed your job to the best of your ability.

6. God won't ask how many friends you had, He'll ask how many people to whom you were a friend.

7. God won't ask what neighborhood you lived, He'll ask how you treated your neighbors.

8. God won't ask about the color of your skin, He'll ask about the content of your character.

9. God won't ask why it took you so long to seek Salvation, He'll lovingly take you to your mansion in Heaven, and not to the gates of Hell.

10. God won't have to ask how many people you shared the Gospel with, He already knows whether or not you were ashamed to share His Word and who you shared it with.

- Modified

Security Ministry

Considering the recent and often mass shootings throughout our country, the Elders of the congregation assigned Kenneth Houston the responsibility to head up a security team along with a plan to keep our congregation safe.

Our primary goal has always been to keep our church family safe.

- Kenneth Houston

Every time the doors are open, you will find this servant-hearted man at the front door usually with his iPad scanning our entrances and exits. He brings his expertise to us with 25 years experience with the Kansas City, MO Police Department to keep us safe during our Worship to God.

One of the first people you will see when coming in the front door of our building is E. J. Smith. He will great you with a smile, give you a handshake, and hand you a bulletin. This man also takes care of our building and grounds, and is our Worship Coordinator. E. J. and Dayon came to us in August 2011 from Southern Oklahoma. They jumped right in with the work here at CoCWH.

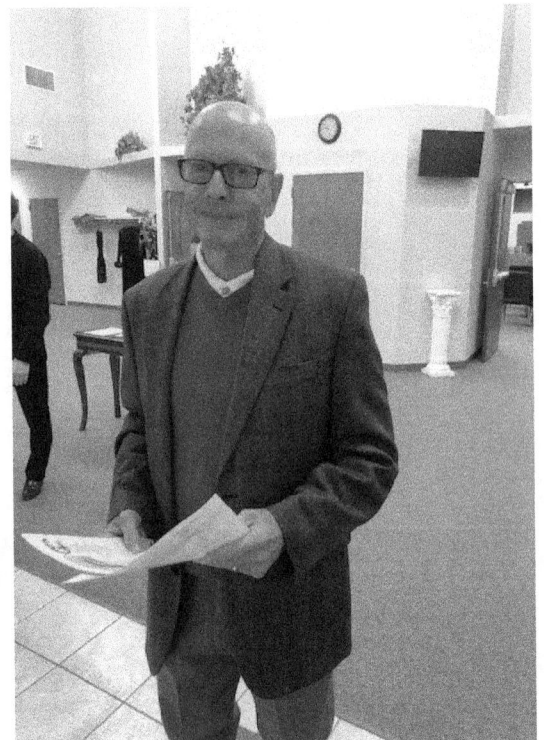

Visitation Ministry

The work of the Lord's church falls into one of three categories, Evangelism, Benevolence, or Edification. There's a quiet small group of Christians at Whispering Hills who are actively involved in the good work of Edification toward the Whispering Hills congregation.

Within the work of Edification, comes the good work of visitation. This small quiet group of concerned members makes up the Whispering Hills Visitation Group. It is the goal of this work to lift up and to encourage one another through needed visits. We try to help one another by providing personal support and assistance of various kinds when needed. Those members who are dealing with health issues at times needs support and assistance. Home and hospital visits are made to encourage and to strengthen one another in their times of need. Meals are made and taken to many who have been hospitalized from accidents, illnesses, and surgeries. Sometimes transportation is needed to go to the doctor or to have treatments, house cleaning if the member is unable to do it themselves. Yard work may be a need that can be taken care of. Help with medicines, this can be confusing and troubling for some and this small group can step in and provide the needed assistance.

Visitation of visitors to our worship services is a part of this group's duties. If we have some visitors who are just passing through on their way home, we greet them hoping to make them feel welcome and at home. Encouragement cards are mailed out to each one of these, thanking them for worshiping with us.

We are very happy to have visitors from our local community come and worship with us. We greet them hoping to make them feel welcome and comfortable with their visit. We attempt to follow up with a visit if possible, if not, then a phone call is made and an encouragement card is mailed out.

If anyone is interested in being a part of this small group of Christians, please contact one of our elders.

- Joe Kelley

Heb 10:24-26

"And let us think of one another and how we can encourage one another to love and do good deeds.

And let us not hold aloof from our church meetings, as some do. Let us do all we can to help one another's faith."

- Phillip's Translation

Women's Ministry

Clothing and More Swap

Do you have things you no longer want or need? Share your items with others and take home things you could use! Swap your stuff.

Clean out your closets and donate gently used women's, men's, and children's clothing as well as shoes, purses, jewelry, and other small household items, etc. All items left after the swap will be donated. Rebecca LeDoux and Kara Snider are in charge of this ministry.

Scheduling Help

As we have many elderly people in our congregation, several need transportation to and from doctor's visits, procedures, etc. There is a group of several ladies of this congregation who provide this much needed help. Faye Ellis does a much needed ministry by scheduling people to transport one of our couples to and from dialysis. Others take on the responsibility of scheduling other needs as they arise.

Sewing Group - Margaret's Missions

Our mother-in-law, Margaret Teakell, was a long time participant and supporter of Tulsans for Life organization. She's done a lot over the years. One of the things I remember is that she was in charge of organizing the schedules and running the pro-life booth at the yearly Tulsa State Fair. Andrea and I got to participate in it a little bit. Our mother-in-law was especially fond of Margaret Hudson's School and loved the fact that the girls there made a pro-life choice.

A week after her funeral, Carolyn Kuzler approached Andrea and me and told us that the ladies of the Church formed a sewing group and named it Margaret's Missions after our mother-in-law. She asked if we wanted to participate. We were honored and touched.

Ever since, we've been mostly sewing for Margaret Hudson's girls, anything for babies and moms. We made burp cloths and bibs, blankets, mini quilts, washcloths, reusable nursing pads, and bags of many designs, from totes with pockets to over the shoulder strap bags. Our goal was to make a different bag for Christmas, enough for every girl in the program, and we filled them with baby items and other gifts. We've also provided a monthly care package of a tote bag filled with baby items and personal hygiene items for mom and baby to be given to their Student of the Month. JoAnn Graham crocheted beautiful baby blankets that were a part of that care package. Carolyn introduced us to the idea of making things for the elderly, she's been our contact to deliver our items to the nursing homes in the area. We made walker bags, feeding bibs, bib scarves, and lap blankets for them. We made dresses for the Little Dresses for Africa program. One time girls from the Bible Class helped us to make bandanas and collar flowers to donate to the Broken Arrow Animal Shelter.

Recently Margaret Hudson's School closed down because they couldn't get enough funding to keep it running as a private school. We will be making more items to donate to the Little Dresses for Africa program, dresses and this time, feminine sanitary pads. I am exploring making reusable cloth diapers and inserts for a baby orphanage in Ukraine that a good Christian friend from my home congregation in Ukraine recommended as needing help.

Our story goes on.

- Lyuba Teakell

Exercise in "Fruitility"

Would you like to improve the way you look at life, others, and yourself? Try this for **two weeks** and see for yourself the difference it will make.

1. Each morning when you wake up, before you get out of bed and start the day, think of five things that you are really thankful to God for, **and then tell Him.**

2. When you get up and look in the mirror, take a big deep breath, look yourself in the eye, smile and say, "I belong to God and He loves me."

3. Before you say the prayer thanking God for your food, think of three people that really need prayers . . . Then pray for them.

4. When you get your breakfast, go get your Bible and feed your mind! Turn to the book of Proverbs and read the first five verses (the second day read the next five, the third day . . . Well, you get the idea). As you eat your meal, read them over and over, and think about the meaning. If you eat breakfast with your mate or children, read together and then talk about the message in the verses and how it applies to each of you today.

5. As you leave for school, work, chores, etc., say to yourself, "I am going to make a difference in someone's life today," and then treat everyone you meet as though this is the last day you will live on this earth.

6. At the close of the day, having done these things, be sure to put your Bible on the table so it will be there when you eat breakfast tomorrow. Say out loud, "This is the day that the LORD has made; let us rejoice and be glad in it." (Psalm 118:24). Pray and go to sleep knowing that God gives His beloved sleep.

Youth Ministry

Over the years, many of the youth have attended church camp at both Quartz Mountain Christian Camp and Burnt Cabin Christian Camp. Several young men have attended the Future Preachers Camp while several young ladies have also attended. Many types of fellowship opportunities have been organized for the youth including regular Teen Devos, group outings to local activities, service projects for members of the congregation, lock-ins, etc.

Daniel Hodges, one of our Deacons, oversees this work, with the help of parents and others.

Annual Girls' Brunch

Honoring our Graduates

Leadership Training for Christ

Youth Activities

Service Projects

Graduate Girls' Brunch

Each year, the Teen Age Girls' Class holds a brunch in honor of our graduate girls in the home of Lori Wooten. It is a special time to honor, love, and encourage our girls to remain faithful to God as they prepare the next stage of their lives. Graduates from past years are also encouraged to attend. We often tell the girls that when they come to our class, they are automatically "Our Girls." Unfortunately, we failed to get pictures every year.

Honoring
Kelsey Coday
&
Bailie Putman
2013 Grads

Honoring
Taylor Lee
&
Makayla Dreiling
2018 Grads

We believe in honoring our High School graduates, and sending them off with a challenge and charge to always remain faithful to God in attendance and service to others. Our Elders also present them with a Bible of their own choosing. Our very first graduates were Ashley Copelin and Joe Rentie who graduated from Broken Arrow High School on May 15, 2003.

A party celebrating their achievements was held in the home of Bob and Ida Stover. We celebrated the occasion by sharing a meal together and then having a special cake decorated for them. After we were in our building, we started the tradition of having each graduate display a table portraying their achievements. This is always a special time to honor them with a fellowship meal.

Honoring our Graduates

Whispering Hills
High School Graduates

2003 - Ashley Copelin, Joe Rentie

2009 - Lauren Parrott, Nick Qualls

2010 - Alex Schriner

2011 - Cory Ben Berna, Travis Kaiser, Jett Mudge, Kayci Snider

2012 - Aaron Collins, Levi Copelin, Nick Dreiling, Kelsey Parrott, Connor Sampson,
Joshua VanTuyl

2013 - Kelsey Coday, Bailie Putman

2014 - Sarah Bates, Lane Denton, Aaron Mitchell, Shawna Robertson, Austin Whittaker,
Hunter Copelin, Madison Kaiser, Kristen VanTuyl

2015 - Madison Fike

2016 - Calee Putman, Griffin Qualls, Cordell Roberson

2017 - Addison Coday, Justin Chandler, Hannah Collins, Aaron Parrott,
Grayson Snider, Josie VanTuyl

2018 - Makayla Dreiling, Taylor Lee

College Graduates

2014 - Connor Sampson, Associate Degree, TCC

2014 - Lauren Parrott, BS, Harding University
Masters in Counseling & Psychology

2016 - Kelsey Parrott, BA, Oklahoma Christian University
Grad School at Oklahoma State University

Travis Kaiser, BS, University of Central Oklahoma
Presently at OU Medical School

2016 - Kayci Snider, BA, Central State University

2018 - Madison Kaiser, BS, University of Central Oklahoma

Other Education

2015 - Aaron Collins- Business Office Technology
2018 – Airframe & Power Plant – Tulsa Tech

2016 – Caleb Collins– Home Builder's Institute
Fork Lift Driving License
Working toward Airframe & Power Plant License – Tulsa Tech

2017 - Kelsey Coday - Airframe & Power Plant

Addison Coday – Working toward Nursing Degree at TCC

2018 – Sarah Bates – Security/Protective Services - Guthrie Job Corp
Now working at Tulsa County Sheriffs Office

I had hoped to have information on the rest of our High School Graduates in order to make this more complete, but was unable to obtain. lw

Leadership for Christ

From puppets

to chorus, there is a place
for all to grow in God's
Service!

LTC Small Chorus

2017: Makayla Dreiling, Josie VanTuyl, Noah Shriner, Justin Chandler and Aaron Parrott

2018: Sydni Ryan, Corrie Ann Bates, Joshua Mitchell, Blake Coday, Justin Chandler, Makayla Dreiling, Christina Welch, Josie VanTuyl, Brooke Ryan, and Drew Morris

Service Projects

Girls' Class Activities

Girls' Teen Class Making
Cookies to Send
College Students

Youth Serve Dinner to our Seniors

Cleaning the Building

When we were first in our new building, the members took turns cleaning it each week. Among those who took a turn was our Youth Group.

Youth Activities

Our Young Men Leading Worship

We at Whispering Hills are very fortunate in having several young men who step up to lead in our worship services. These are just a few of them.

1. Top Left - Blake Coday, graduating Senior, leading singing
2. Top - Joshua Mitchell, Junior, preaching a sermon
3. Hunter Copelin, young professional, leading singing

Zone Groups

After going through variations of this, we have settled on a grouping of the members according to where they live. There are four Zones with about 25 families in each one. Two families are set up as the leaders of each of the Zones. They coordinate the providing of food for families that have gone through sicknesses, deaths, or other needs. The leaders also provide leadership in setting up the dinners we have every other month and the special activities (egg hunt, 4th of July, Fall Festival), and helping with the needs of the families in their Zones. This really allows for the congregation as a whole to do a lot of good.

- Dale Graham

Zone Meeting at Shirley Lumpkin's Home

Zone Meeting at Bob & Ida Stover's Home

Shirley Lumpkin, Louise Adams, Diana & Jerry Spradley, Joyce Foster, Margaret Campbell, Kathy Cox, and Dee Koons

Death - A Wonderful Way to Explain It

A sick man turned to his doctor as he was preparing
to leave the examination room and said,
"Doctor, I am afraid to die. Tell me what lies on the other
side."
Very quietly, the doctor said, "I don't know. . . "
"You don't know? You're a Christian man,
and don't know what's on the other side?"
The doctor was holding the handle of the door;
on the other side came a sound of scratching and whining,
and as he opened the door, a dog sprung into the room
and leaped on him with an eager show of gladness.
Turning to the patient, the doctor said,
"Did you notice my dog?
He's never been in this room before.
He didn't know what was inside.
He knew nothing except that his master was here,
and when the door opened, he sprang in without fear.
I know little of what is on the other side of death,
but I do know one thing . . .
I know my Master is there and that is enough."

Church of Christ at Whispering Hills

Broken Arrow, Oklahoma

Section Three

Leadership

Elders
Ministers
Deacons

Getting to Know our Current Elders

Wayne Ford (2015-Present)

Wayne was born in Logansport, IN and raised in Farmers Branch, TX. He graduated from James Madison High Scholl, Houston, TX in 1973. He attended Sam Houston State University and then attended and graduated from Sunset School of Preaching in 1976. He married Sandra Talbott in Houston, TX in 1977. He worked in "retail" for 7 years and then enlisted in the U. S. Navy in 1983. He retired in 2004, worked with the U.S. Government for 12 years with the U.S. Air Force at Malmstrom AFB in Great Falls, MT and then moved to Broken Arrow, OK to work with the Bureau of Land Management. He officially retired in 2018.

Over numerous years, they assisted local congregations in numerous ways including teaching, Youth Minister, Associate Minister, and Evangelist. He and Sandra have 3 children and 6 grandchildren. They have been members at Whispering Hills since 2012 and became an Elder in 2015.

Tony grew up in Idabel, OK, graduating from High School in 1970. He was baptized there at the age of 12. He received a BSE degree from Oklahoma Christian University in 1974. While at OC he met Marcia Adams from Topeka Kansas and they were married on August 7, 1974. He taught in public schools in Midwest City, Oklahoma for three years, and worked as a Manufacturer's Agent for several years before starting his own Agency in 1982 (Lightsey Marketing).

Tony and Marcia have two children and five grandchildren. They have been members at Whispering Hills since 2006. He became an Elder in 2010. He along with our other Elders take turns preaching when our Pulpit Minister is unavailable.

Tony Lightsey (2010 - Present)

Steve Parrott is a CPA with a Masters in Finance from Texas A & M University. Much of his secular work experience has been in the energy, public accounting, and banking industries. He and Martha met at the beginning of their college years at the 29th and Yale Church of Christ where Martha's father was a minister. They attended Oklahoma Christian and married the summer following their college graduation. While at Oklahoma Christian, they developed together a love for mission work and were part of a group which established the Lord's Church in Wimbledon, England. Martha completed her doctoral degree from Oklahoma State University and is a Professor of Mathematics and university administrator. Her focus is on teacher training with undergraduate and graduate students. Steve, Martha, and children began worshiping with the Whispering Hills congregation the first day the were opened at our current site, June 6, 2004. Since that time, they have virtually served in every area of service. Having been appointed to serve as a deacon, Steve was asked by the Elders to

Steve Parrott (2012 - Present)

design and implement the first Whispering Hills Visitation and Brothers' Keeper service opportunities. They have devoted many years of service to our youth through teaching and Leadership Training for Christ as well as our college students and young adults. In 2012, Steve accepted the invitation to serve as an Elder. Martha serves faithfully by his side having taught classes of all ages including the young ladies and women of the congregation. Their children and spouses are all faithful servants in the Lord's church.

Mike Snider is originally from Duncan, Oklahoma. He grew up in the household of an Elder of the Lord's church. He is married to his wife Judy and has two sons, Greg Snider and Blake Snider. He and his wife have four grandchildren and two daughters-in-law.

Mike has a degree in Physics and Chemistry and has done graduate work at Eastern New Mexico University, New Mexico Institute of Technology, and New Mexico State University. He has worked as a public school teacher and was Vice President of the Teletraining Institute located at Oklahoma State University. He also was owner and President of his consulting firm. Mike has served as a minister for 24 years and has served as an Elder in three different

Mike Snider (2007 - Present)

Current Elders & Wives

Wayne & Sandra Ford
2015 - Present

Tony & Marcia Lightsey
2010 - Present

Steve & Marth Parrott,
Lauren, Kelsey, Aaron
2012 - Present

Mike & Judy Snider
2007 - 2012
2015 - Present

Former Elders and Wives

Nathan & Pam Bell
2002 - 2008

Jerry & Diana Spradley
2002 - 2008
2012 - 2014

Russel & Margaret Teakell
2009 - 2011

Geames & Lori Wooten
2002 - 2011

Pulpit Ministers & Families

Dan Langdon

Dan Langdon officially became our first pulpit Minister in August 2004. He and wife, Kathy, had been missionaries first in Japan for two years, and then in Scotland for six years. In January 1999, they moved to Glenrothes, Scotland and were there six years. In March of 2004, the Langdons came to the states to find a position at home as they desired to be closer to their aging parents.

They have four children: Liem, Abby, Levi, and Anna Grace. They came to Whispering Hills while we were meeting in the Senior Citizens Center with Dan preaching both lessons. The Wootens had a fellowship for them Sunday night after evening worship and everyone loved them. The Elders had not planned to hire a minister that soon, but decided they would go ahead and look into the possibility of hiring Dan, as they felt he and his family would attract young families. Dan, Kathy, and Anna Grace were present on our first day of worship on June 6, 2004. We continued to grow.

Dan & Kathy Langdon,
Liam, Abby, Levi, Anna Grace
2004 - 2007

91

Dale Graham

Dale & JoAnn Graham
2008 - Present

Dale was born 24 Nov. 1954 in Ohio. He graduated from Harding University with a B.A. in Bible and Biblical Languages in 1976.

He has preached in Arkansas, Missouri, and Kentucky.

He came to Whispering Hills in January of 2008.

He is married to JoAnn and they have three grown boys.

JoAnn is a talented preschool teacher and actively supports her husband in all of his work.

They both love the Lord and His Word.

His objectives in his own words:

- God's Word is the power of God.

- I preach textual lessons. I want the members to know what the Bible says, not what I think.

- I enjoy teaching and want to be involved in the Bible classes.

- I believe that elders have the oversight of a congregation and that they set the direction of the congregation (within God's Word).

- I use Power Point to teach and preach.

- I recognize the impact of making visits to the hospital, nursing homes, and wherever I am needed.

*Finally, brethren,
whatever things are true,
whatever things are noble,
whatever things are just,
whatever things are pure,
whatever things are lovely,
whatever things are of good report,
if there is any virtue
and if there is anything
praiseworthy—
meditate on these things.*

Philippians 4:8 NKJV

Current Deacons & Wives

Eddie & Linda Bates
2003 - Present

Charles & April Bower
2012 - Present

Brian & Kristi Chandler
2012 - Present

Clif & Carol Dreiling
2005 - Present

Daniel & Jenny Hodges
2008 - Present

Earl & Jan Laney
2012 - Present

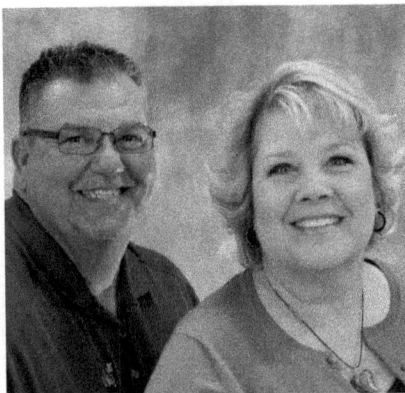

Larry & Jil Shackelford
2012 - Present

E J & Dayon Smith
2012 - Present

Greg & Kara Snider
2005 - Present

Previous Deacons & Wives

Ed & Kathy Buchanan
2005 - 2008

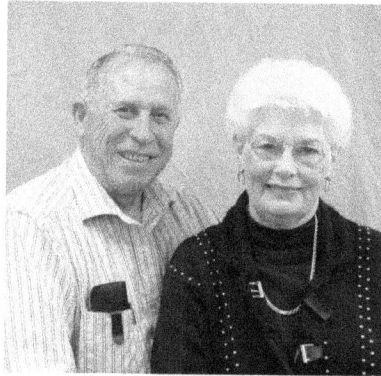

Lawrence & Barbara Buckner
2003 - 2012

David & Karen Foster
2005 - 2017

Vernon & Kanna Guess
2005 - 2009

Tony & Marcia Lightsey
2008 - 2010

Steve & Martha Parrott
2005 - 2012

Carlton & Doris Pittman
2012 - 2012

Everett & Letha Putman
2003 - 2006

Ed & Martha Rentie
2003 - 2006

Previous Deacons & Wives, Cont'd

Ron & Lorna Schriner
2008 - 2008

Walter & Regina Sorrell
2003 - 2012

Bob & Ida Stover
2003 - 2014

Russell & Margaret Teakell
2003 - 2009

Joe & Melissa VanTuyl
2012 - 2017

My Gratitude

For loved ones You have given me,
For friends I cannot number,
For Blood which daily cleanses me,
For nightly peaceful slumber;

For work to do, for love to share,
For burdens often lifted,
For open hearts and open doors
And help from those more gifted;

For guidance of the Living Word,
And comfort of the Spirit
For intercession at Thy throne
When prayer shall bring me near it;

For confidence that others give,
For trust they place within me;
For godly souls who for You live,
And strength they ever lend me;

For steadfast souls who stand the shock
When Satan fiercely assails them,
Whose feet are firm upon the Rock
Where you do never fail them;

For peace and calm amid the storm,
For lessons learned through failing;
For faith that o'er the evil yet
The good will be prevailing;

For crown and throne and golden home
And life when life shall end,
I thank you, Father, Lord of all,
In Jesus name. Amen

- Selected

Church of Christ at Whispering Hills

Broken Arrow, Oklahoma

Section Four

Miscellaneous

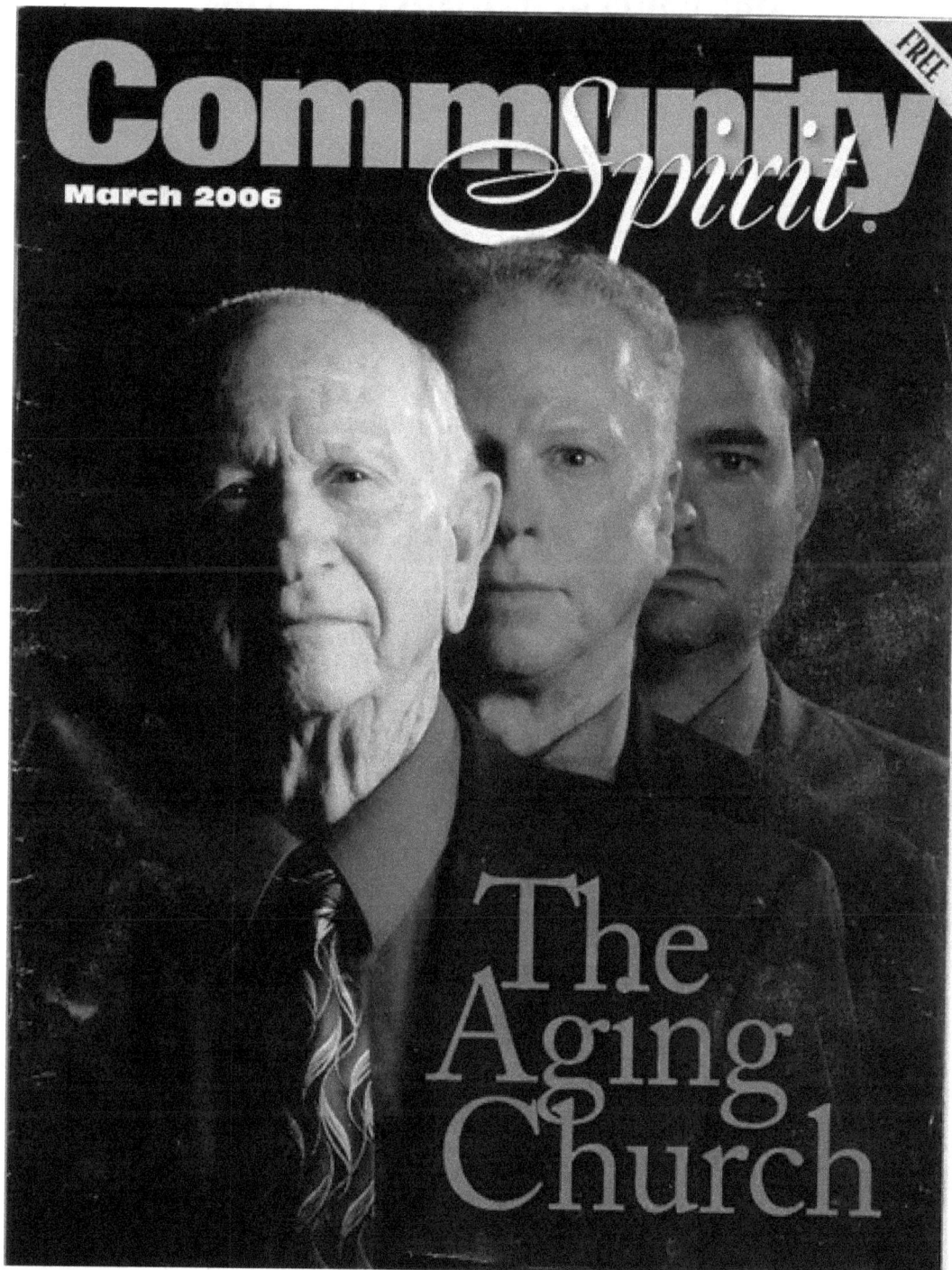

3 Generations: Virgil, Nolen, & Jeremy Harris

Baptisms at Whispering Hills

Dee Koons, 4.22.03
Lawrence Buckner, 5.18.2003
Winnie Matthews, 5.18.2003
Everett Putnam, 5.18.2003
Letha Putnam, 5.18.2003
Phil Kidd, 10.8.2003
Nicole Kidd, 10.8.2003
Elizabeth Carter, 11.8.2003
Kristi Kemp, 1.7.2004
Clayton Morris, 9.11.2004
Sherry Morris, 9.11.2004
John Casey, 10.19.2004
Deannie Casey, 10.19.2004
Kayci Snider, 3.6.2005
Teresa Sparks, 4.29.2005
Gene Dunham, 6.21.2005
Beckett Killam, 6.27.2005
Kristen Legg, 6.28.2005
Josh Laney, 6.28.2005
Troy Spillers, 7.22.2005
Belinda Spillers, 7.22.2005
Christina Yaws, 12.14.2005
Kelsey Parrott, 12.14.2005
Tucker Karman, 1.8.2006
Ken Winters, 2.15.2006
Kent Hale, 5.2.2006
Elizabeth Fowler, 5.27.2007
Aaron Mitchell, 11.25.2007
Nick Middleton, 6.8.2008
Kerri Julian, 7.17.2008
Travis Kaiser, 9.22.2008
Levi Copeland, 1.14.2009
Nicole Brown, 8.2.2009
Trent Bennett, 9.20.2009
Sarah Bates, 9.23.2009
Vern Guess, 11.22.2009
Roberta Guess, 11.22.2009
Callie Putnam, 12.6.2009
Bailie Putnam, 12.13.2009
Jett Mudge, 4.5.2010
Charlsie Kreeley, 6.10.2010
Kelsey Coday, 6.23.2010
Timothy Collins, 7.19.2010
Hannah Collins, 7.21.2010
Hunter Copelin, 8.22.2010
Nick Dreiling, 8.22.2010

Aaron Parrott, 1.3.2011
Chris Bragg, 4.17.2011
Seth Bragg, 7.19.2011
Connor Sampson, 8.7.2011
Andrew Gilpin, 8.28.2011
Dicie Putnam, 9.28.2011
Cody Buckner, 10.5.2011
Amanda Saunders, 10.5.2011
Courtney Listen, 10.16.2011
Tom Lorincz, 3.11.2012
Larry Buckner, 4.22.2012
Natasha Allen, 4.29.2012
Joshua VanTuyl, 4.29.2012
Caleb Collins, 10.21.2012
Eric Henry, 12.2.2012
Gary McWherter, 5.19.2013
Grayson Snider, 7.28.2013
Joshua Mitchell, 2.9.2014
Gracie Sampson, 2.14.2014
Autumn Chase, 2.16.2014
Josie VanTuyl, 6.16.2014
Makayla Dreiling, 7.6.2014
Madison Kaiser, 7.15.2014
Brooke Ryan, 12.28.2014
Elisa Coday, 6.21.2015
Blake Coday, 7.5.2015
Addison Coday, 7.5.2015
Sydni Ryan, 9.14.2015
Erica Coday, 1.17.2016
Taylor Lee, 6.16.2016
Phoenix LeDoux, 6.17.2016
Katie Collins, 10.2.2016
Pete Poulos, 10.25.2016
Dennis Ward, 2.7.2017
Kayci Guess, 3.19.2017
Avery VanTuyl, 3.29.2017
Bobby Evans, 4.2.2017
Steven Sisney, 4.2.2017
Noah Denton, 6.7.2017
Greg Cobb, 6.18.2017
Cecilia Marlin, 8.20.2017
Audrey Little, 3.25.2018
Corrie Ann Bates, 4.9.2018
Drew Morris, 6.8.2018
Sterling LeDoux, 6.8.2018
Mary Nelson, 7.8.2018
Christina Welch, 9.23.2018

In Loving Memory

Jay Adams, January 25, 2003
Judy Bates, January 30, 2005
Jeane Freeman, December 5, 2005
Roy Priest, December 24, 2005
Evelyn Barthel, April 24, 2008
Dan McCarty, January 11, 2009
Patsy Messick, August 6, 2009
Kent Hale, Margaret Campbell's Son, June 2, 2010
Cledith Snider, Mike Snider's Mother, June 7, 2010
Thurman Caywood, October 29, 2010
Margaret Teakell, January 23, 2011
Geames Wooten, February 27, 2011
Winnie Matthews, April 19, 2011
Kathryn Priest, May 19, 2011
Bud Messick, April 20, 2012
Imogene Browning, December 18, 2012
Logan Bower, December 24, 2012
Beth Johnson, February 21, 2013
Claudette Hudelson, May 23, 2013
Lawrence Buckner, August 3, 2013
Daril Thompson, 12.16.2013
Melvin Harmon, July 2, 2014
Russell Teakell, August 30, 2014
Louise Adams, February 4, 2015
Shelby McCarty, May 9, 2015
Verlin Embrey, May 13, 2015
David Sampson, August 26, 2015
Don Bragg, January 25, 2016
Carol Pennington, July 3, 2016
Bobby Evans, May 2, 2017
Judith Tackett, May 3, 2017
Genelle Harris, May 15, 2017
Doug Aitkenhead, October 29, 2027
Oliver Coffman, November 20, 2017
Howard Tackett, January 8, 2018
Noah Lars Schriner, January 19, 2018
Virgil Harris, July 23. 2018

In Loving Memory of Aunt Bea

Beatrice Stackhouse, "Aunt Bea" to those who knew her, passed from this life Friday, July 13, 2007, at the age of 94. She is survived by her husband, Dan Stackhouse, several nieces, nephews of the Johnston family which include Delores Wilson, Dearl Watson, Winnie Matthews and Jim Cotner of Broken Arrow, Charles Johnston of Richardson, Texas, Ron Johnston of Edmond, Oklahoma and Paula Bradshaw of Oklahoma City, Oklahoma, and a host of friends. Though Sister Stackhouse had no children of her own, she is loved and claimed by countless many as "Aunt Bea". She is best known for her love of the Lord, Jesus Christ and His church. She loved to sing the hymns of the church, as did her parents and siblings. Her two brothers, the late Versal L. Johnston and the late Paul F. Johnston were both gospel preachers in various churches of Christ in Oklahoma. She painted in oils and those close to her received one or more of her beautiful paintings.

The Johnston homestead still stands as part of the property now owned by Whispering Hills members, John & Deanie Casey and Geames & Lori Wooten. It was her dream as a girl that one day there would be a church meeting on her daddy's property. That reality became fact on June 6, 2004. She lived to see her dream fulfilled and she and Dan were able to be with us the very first Sunday Whispering Hills met on September 1, 2002. She and Dan were also present at the groundbreaking in January 2003 and at the Open House in October 2004.

Bea Stackhouse, Lynna Johnston, Versal Johnston, Gladys Steeley, Winnie Matthews

In Loving Memory

of

Noah Schriner

Words cannot begin to express the loss our congregation felt at the time of Noah's death. There will always be a void because he no longer is with us. Noah was such an exemplary person, far beyond his years. He exemplified the Fruit of the Spirt in his life (Galatians 5). He was a servant to all, and especially to the older generations as he would spend time helping them with things like washing windows or whatever was needed. He would not accept pay for his service. He was truly a servant of God, even at such a young age.

As Noah shared his faith in God and in life, we of the church of Christ at Whispering Hills shared God's glory in Noah's death. So many friends and family have talked about how special our church family is and how wonderful our singing and scriptural reliance was.

Noah was behind this pulpit many times and always gave thought producing lessons. He was a very versatile person with many talents. Whether he was in the pulpit, playing his instrument in the Pride, or helping others, he always did his best. He was SPECIAL! He will always be in our hearts.

Noah loved preaching and he loved being in the Pride!

Miscellaneous Pictures

Who ever said
Christians don't
have fun!

Miscellaneous Pictures

Roz Evans (Center) Visiting From
Australia Shown with Rae
Parette & Lori Wooten

Ashley Copelin's Bridal Shower

Melanie Coday & Claudette Hudelson at
Desera Shackelford's Bridal Shower

Vicki Kelley, one of our ladies who
work at the Welcome Booth before
Class & Worship on Sunday mornings.

The Blooming Ladies

Winnie Matthews had received a corsage from a piano student and wore it several times, so we decided that one Wednesday night we would all wear corsages. What fun!

Kara Snider & Cindy Sampson

Great

Memories!

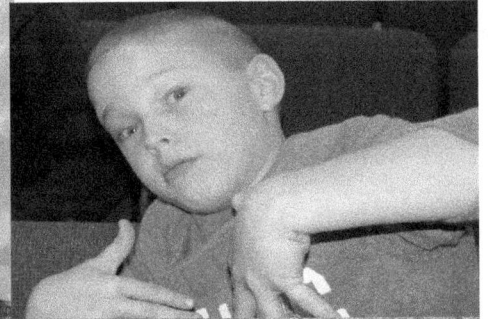

Pic 1: Chase's grandchildren with Geames
         Wooten
Pic 2: Grayson Snider
Pic 3: Bea Stackhouse in front of bull dozier
Pic 4: Camping at Blue Bill: Mike & Judy
         Snider, Kathy Langdon
Pic 5: Camping: Sue Doss (BA), Lori Wooten,
         Mike & Judy Snider, Rae Parette

Young and Old,
We Are FAMILY!

Pic 1: Elisa Coday
Pic 2: Charles Parette & J. J. Bragg
Pic 3: Dale Graham & Hayride
Pic 4: Dan Langdon w/Egg Hunters
Pic 5: Dale Graham & Greg Snider
      Hayrides

In 2003, Winnie Matthews, deceased wife of Glen, purchased these dresses for our very young ladies. Aren't they precious!

**Kayci Snider, Kayelynn Chase, Bailie Putman, Sarah Bates,
Abigail Parette, August Rain Matthews,
Calee Putman, and Jenna Kidd**

**Happy New Year's
Eve Party**

Adalyn Hodges

Fun and Fellowship

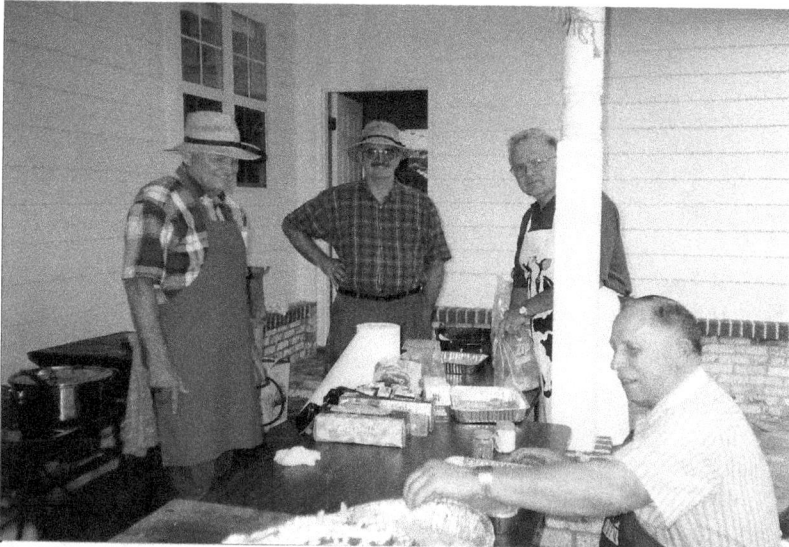

Left - Fish Fry at Wooten's

Below - Fall Festival
Hay Ride

Hayride Anyone?

Geames Wooten would tell the riders to be quiet until he waved his hat, then they could yell and scream as loud as they wanted. . .they loved it!

Judy Tackett seems to be having a really good time!

Fall Festival 2017

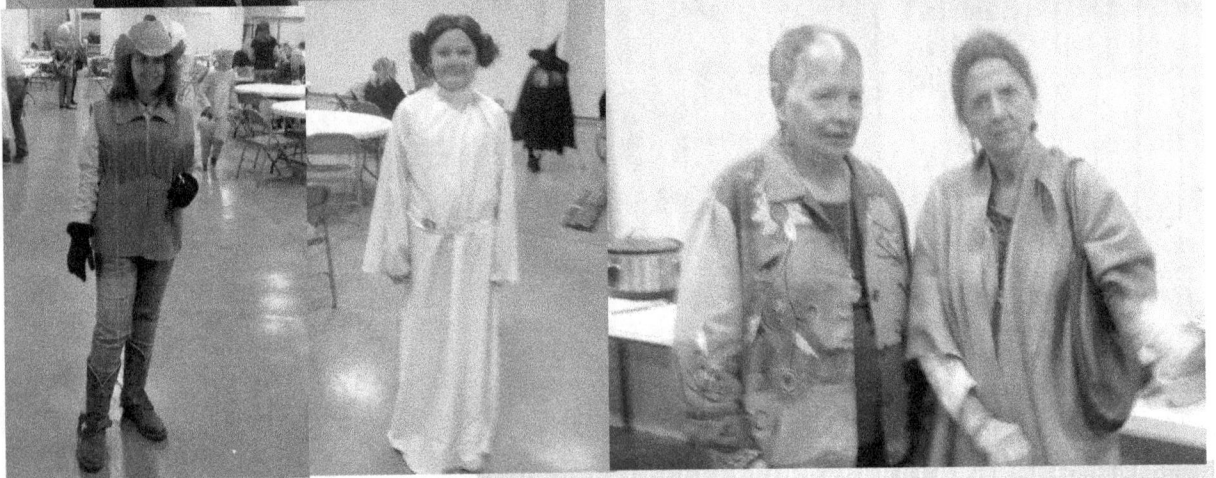

Picture 1: Deborah Houston & Marjory
Picture 2: Jett & Jerry Marlin
Picture 3: Desera & Jon Shackleford
Picture 4: Hannah Collins
Picture 5: Phoenix LeDoux
Picture 6: Joy Ellis & Rae Parette
Picture 7: Dale Graham's Hayride

Fall Festival 2018

Picture 1: Adalyn Hodges, Ryan
          Morris, & Luiz Orozco
Picture 2: Hannah & Felicity Bower
Picture 3: Patti Thompson & Lori
          Wooten
Picture 4: Carter Shackelford
Picture 5: Jace Shackelford

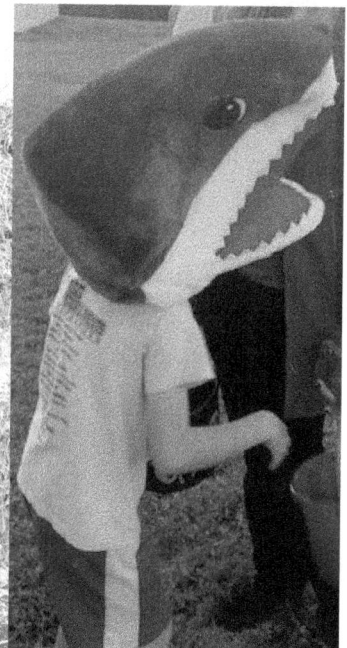

Fall Festival 2018, Cont'd

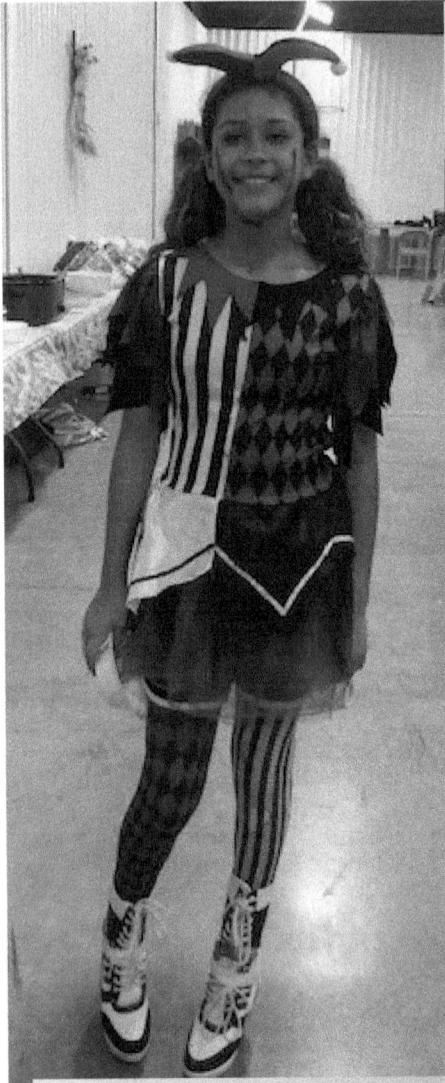

Picture 1: Ryan Morris
Picture 2: Chuck Ellis &
      Mark Messick
Picture 3: Desera Shackelford
Picture 4: VanTuyl Family
Picture 5: Carter Shackelford
      & Felicity Bower

Fall Festival 2018, Cont'd

Picture 1: Lilly & Ron Schriner
Picture 2: Jon Shackelford Family
Picture 3: Pat Lewis & Son
Picture 4: Mark & Jessica Ford's
             Family

Church of Christ at Whispering Hills

Broken Arrow, Oklahoma

Section Five

Time Line

Whispering Hills Time Line

1999

- Bea and Dan Stackhouse first mentioned gift of 20 acres.

2000

- July 24, 2000, The Stackhouses wrote letter to Broken Arrow Church of Christ telling of desire to donate 20 acres for establishing a congregation of the Lord's people in Southeast Broken Arrow.

- On August 27, 2000, Bill Rampey, now deceased, made the announcement before morning worship about the wonderful opportunity that the new congregation would be for the South part of Broken Arrow and the Wagoner County area.

2001

- During the Elders Planning Session in February 2001, one item on the agenda was to begin planning for the new congregation; so long-range plans for the property, which is now Whispering Hills, began.

2002

- Take a City Group #8 began planning for new congregation in January with monthly meetings continuing.

- A letter was sent to the Broken Arrow congregation, written by Gerry Lynn for the Elders on February 14, 2002, to form an evangelistic support group.

- Whispering Hills began as a congregation September 1, 2002, in the Senior Citizens Center at 1800 S. Main Street, and continued meeting there until our building was completed June 6, 2004.

- Geames & Lori Wooten's 40th Wedding Anniversary

- First Ladies Bible Class met September 8, 2002 in home of Rae Parette.

- Elders ordained October 6, 2002.
-
- Planning session at Wootens.

2003

- Ground Breaking and deed presented to our Elders on January 3, 2003

- Pre-construction began.

- First High School graduates: Ashley Copeland & Joe Rentie, honored at Bob & Ida Stovers.

- The first speaker who presented a gospel lesson on the present site was Riley Killam, grandson of Charles and Rae Parette, on a Wednesday night in June or July 2003.

- The gas line was already on 111th, but water had to be brought across the street. Rod Copelin and crew took care of bringing the water line under the 211th and onto the property. Several men of the congregation helped.

- 10.02.2003 - Air Balloon & Geames' Birthday Party at Howard & Judy Tacketts

2004

- 04.04.2004 - Dan Langdon and family, Kathy, Liem, Abby, Levi, Anna Grace visit. The Elders had not planned to hire a minister that soon, but decided after much prayer and planning that they would go ahead and hire Dan.

- 06.06.2004 - Dan Langdon preached for our first worship service in completed building on June 6, 2004. The Langdons came from Scotland and also looked for a house.

- 10.17.2003 - Open House on October 17, 2004

- Men's Leadership Class began. Met on first and third Thursday of each month.

- 11.28.2004 - Steve, Martha, Laura, Kelsey, Aaron Parrott placed membership

2005

- 04.03.2005 - New Deacons Selected: Ed Buchanan, Clif Dreiling, Steve Parrott, David Sampson, Greg Snider

- 4.08.2005 - Movie Night with dinner and showing "Gospel of John."

- 4.26.2005 - Housewarming for Craig Wooten

- 4.30.2005 - Ladies Day with Marcia Lightsey, Speaker

- 5.21.2005 - Family Fun Day at the Zoo

- 5.24.2005 - Andrea Davis Bridal Shower, bride elect of Kevin Teakell

- 6.04.2005 - Micah & Lisa Waldroop's mission trip to El Salvadore

- 6.26.2005 - Burnt Cabin Youth Camp

- 7.03.2005 - All church picnic & fireworks at Foster-Guess Residence

- 7.31.2005 - Ed Rentie, Grant Teakell & Lyuba Petrova return to Ukraine

- 8.24.2005 - Boys' Class held wordship service at Coweta, OK congregation. Girls' Class went to lend their support.

- 9.04.2005- Katrina Relief—The entire contribution from previous week was sent to White's Ferry Road Church of Christ for Katrina Hurricane victims. A portion of this weeks's contribution will also be sent. Helped Broken Arrow congregation sort clothes and other items; and also helped Coweta congregation pay for fuel to take two semis to Gulf Port, MS.

- 9.11.2005 - New Converts Class began with Jerry Spradley and Geames Wooten.

- 10.09.2005 - Youth to do chores for elderly. Contact David Martin and Greg Snider

- 10.20.2005- Fall Campout at Blue Bill Campground

- 10.29.2005 - Our young people are looking for projects to do on October 29. If you need your guttering cleaned out or leaves picked up, etc., please call Ed Rentie

- 10.29.2005 - Good Guy Carnival, Game Night & Hayride

- 11.20.2005 - Stephen Bates awarded custody of Corrie Anne

- 12.04.2005 - Participated in Angel Tree – The daughter of Virgil & Genelle Harris works at the OU – Tulsa on the IMPACT team. The team of doctors, nurses, and therapists provide services to over 55 adults who suffer from severe mental illness. Most have no family who will associate with them. They live on the street or in bare, cheap apartments. They all have their own unique stories and have made lists of items they want for Christmas. If you would like to adopt one of these "angels," contact Virgil or Genelle for details.

- 12.17.2005 - Grant Teakell and Lyuba Petrova Wedding in Ukraine

- 12.31.2005 - New Year Eve's Game Night and Devo

2006

- 02.12.2006 - Tony and Marcia Lightsey Placed Membership

- 02.18.2006 - Young at Heart Banquet

- 02.19.2006 - Services cancelled because of ice

- 02.26.2006 - Virgil & Genelle Harris' 60th Wedding Anniversary

- 03.03.2006 - Ladies Night Out at Lori Wooten's Home

- 04.21.2006 - Movie Night - Passion of Christ - Adults; Prince of Egypt—Children

- 04.23.2006 - Family Cookout/ Egg Hunt

- 05.28.2006 - Ice Cream Social at the Wootens

- 07.02.2006- All church fellowship at the Fosters

- 11.05.2006 - Food Baskets for Families in Need

- 12. 2005 - Additional Elders' Selection began

- 12.31.2006- New Year Eve's Party

- 12. 2005 - Additional Elders' Selection began

- 12.31.2006- New Year Eve's Party

2007

- 04.15.2007 - Card Shower for Bea Stackhouse

- 04.21.2007- Eagle Scout Project for Broken Arrow

- 6.10.2007 - Ice Cream Social at Wootens

- 07.01.2007 - Foster-Guess 4th of July Celebration

- 07.22.2007 - Jenny Hodges Baby Shower

- 08.24.2007 - Lock-in for 6th Grade and up

- 09.16.2007 - Sherry Morris Baby Shower

- 09.30.2007 - Lorna Schriner Baber Shower

- 10.22.2007 - Joyce Foster Making Quilts for Benevolence

- 10.22.2007 – Good Guy Game Night, Cookout and Hayride

- 11.04.2007 – Dan Langdon want to return as Pulpit Minister

- 11.11.2007 – Jason & Lori Bates Wedding Shower - Reception

- 12.09.2007 - Lyuba Petrova Teakell Bridal Shower

- 12.09.2007 – Walter Buchanan preached

- 12.16.2007 - Dale Graham tried out for Pulpit Minister

- 12.23.2007– Announcement that Dale Graham to be new Pulpit Minister

- 12.31.2007-All church New Year's party

2008

- 01.27.2008 – Dale and JoAnn Graham begin their ministry with us

- 03.02.2008 – Jerry Spradley resigns as Elder

- 03.02.2008 – Dale mails out bulletins to Broken Arrow

- 03.21.2008 – LTC Convention in Rogers, AR – 25 students and adults

- 03.29.2008 – Cookout and Egg Hunt

- 04.13.2008 – New Deacons Appointed: David Foster, Vernon Guess, Daniel Hodges, Tony Lightsey, Ron Schriner

- 04.27.2008 - Kanna Guess Baby Shower

- 05.18.2008 - Elizabeth Fowler Laney Wedding Shower

- 07.06.2008 - Annual 4th of July Celebration at Foster-Guess

- 09.28.2008 - Gospel Meeting with Dale Graham - Ark of the Covenant

- 09.28.2008 - Member's Day

- 09.29.2008 - All church fellowship at Wootens

- 11.02.2008 - Bill Burton preached

- 11.29.2008 - November Food Drive

- 12.26.2008 - Geames Wooten's Horse Accident

- 12.31.2008- New Year's Eve Party

2009

- 01.04.2009 - Mike Snider and Russell Teakell selected as new Elders.

- 05.17.2009 - Graduating Seniors: Lauren Parrott and Nick Qualls

- 08.06.2009 - Patsy Messick passed away

2010

- 06.05.2010 - Glen & Winnie Matthews' 50th Wedding Anniversary

- 10.10.2010 - Tony Lightsey & Jerry Spradley installed as new Elders. Entire Eldership: Tony Lightsey, Jerry Spradley, Russell Teakell, Geames Wooten

- 11.13.2010 - Earl & Jan Laney's 50th Wedding Anniversary

2011

- 01.23.2011 - Margaret Teakell passed away

- 02.20.2011- Russell Teakell resigned as Elder

- 02.25.2011 - Virgil & Genelle Harris' 65th Wedding Anniversary

- 02.27.2011 - Geames Wooten passed away

- 04.19.2011- Winnie Matthews passed away

- 05.19.2011- Katherine Priest passed away

- 05.22.2011- Graduating Seniors: Cory Ben Berna, Travis Kaiser, Jett Mudge

2012

- 01.12.2012 - Steve Parrott ordained as an Elder
  Eldership: Tony Lightsey, Steve Parrott, Jerry Spradley

- 05.06.2012 - Graduating Seniors: Aaron Collins, Levi Copelin, Nick Dreiling, Kelsey Parrott, Conner Sampson

- 07.08.2012– Girls' Class Project for Beth Johnson

- 09.16.2012 - Placed Membership: Daril & Patti Thompson, Ray & Pat Lewis

- 09.30.2012 - Placed Membership: Wayne, Sandra, Emily Ford

- 12.16.2012 - Mike Snider resigned as Elder, later reinstalled

2013

- 03.23.2013- Claudette Hudelson passed away
-
- 08.03.2013 - Lawrence Buckner passed away

- 12.16.2013 - Daril Thompson passed away

2014

- 05.04.2014 - Graduating Seniors: Sarah Bates, Lane Denton, Aaron Mitchell, Shawna Robertson, Austin Whittaker, Hunter Copelin, Madison Kaiser, Kristen VanTuyl
  -
- 05.09.2014 - Connor Sampson received Associates Degree from TCC

- 05.25.2014 - Jerry Spradley resigned as Elder

- 08.30.2014 - Russell Teakell passed away

- 10.05.2014 - Friends and Family Day

2015

- 01.03.2015 - Walter & Regina Sorrell's 50th Wedding Anniversary

- 01.23.2015 - Joe Kelley & Richard Sample's trip to Philippines

- 02.04.2015 - Louise Adams passed away

- 03.13.2015 - Verlin Embry passed away

- 05.03.2015 - Graduating Senior: Madison Fike

- 05.16.2015 - Lauren Parrott & Thomas Bond Wedding

- 08.01.2015 - Collin Teakell & Elizabeth Havenar Wedding

- 08.11.2015 - Card shower for Ethel McCallie - 99th birthday

- 08.26.2015 - David Sampson passed away

- 12.11.2015 - Ethel McCallie passed away

2016

- 02.26.2016 - Virgil & Genelle Harris' 70th Wedding Anniversary

- 03.06.2016 - Friends & Family Day

- 05.01.2016 - Graduating Seniors: Calee Putman, Griffin Qualls, Cordell Roberson

- 07.03.2016 - Carol Pennington passed away

- 07.29.2016 - Aaron Collins & Katie Monroe Wedding

- 10.25.2016 - Pete Poulos baptized into Christ

2017

- 02.05.2017 - 1st Quarter Elders' Emphasis: Attendance

- 04.01.2017 - 2nd Quarter Elders' Emphasis: Evangelism

- 05.03.2017 - Juddith Tackett passed away

- 05. .2017 - Graduating Seniors: Justin Chandler, Addison Coday, Hannah Collins, Aaron Parrott, Grayson Snider, Josie Vantuyl, and Korbin Hershberger

- 06.11.2017 - New Classes: Dale Graham's Sunday morning class - Book of James Harold Tydings - Adult Class in Auditorium - False Teachers & False Doctrines

- 06.14.2017 - Lock - In for 6th - 12th grade

- 07.01.2017 - Third Quarter Elders' Emphasis: Giving

- 07.02.2017 - Independence Day Fellowship, Feast & Fireworks with hayride and horseback riding, volleyball, kickball, softball

- 09.17.2017 - Special contribution of Hurricane Relief

- 09.24.2017 - Military & College Outreach - Each military and college student received a box filled with snacks, candy, and cookies thanks to the generous gifts from so many within the congregation

- 09.24.2017 - Leadership Training for Christ - Students and parents are encouraged to pick up interest survey forms in the foyer and return them to Steve or Martha by September 27.

- 09.24.2017 - Cheryl Bode, Missionary in Charge at the Chimala Mission Hospital, Chimala, Tanzania will be here before and after evening worship.

- 10.01.2017 - 4th Quarter Elders' Emphasis: Family

- 10.01.2007 - Meeting with Noel Whitlock, Pulpit Minister of College Church of Christ, Searcy, AR - Good News From God's Word For Your Family. Topics are: Faith Begins at Home, Fight for your Marriage, Building Marriages that Last, Surviving Tough Times, Priorities in Parenting, Spoiling your Grandchildren.

- 10.28.2017 - Fall Festival - chili contest, costume contest, hayrides, Trunk or Treat, bonfire and hayride for our middle and high schoolers

- 10.22.2017 - Doug Aitkenhead passed away after a long illness. Graveside service was held at Fort Gibson Military Cemetery on November 2 at 2:00 p.m.

- 11.05.2017 - Elders' Report for September and October

  1. Provided contributed funds for hurricane brethren in Houston, TX
  2. Contributed church funds from treasury for relief efforts in TX
  3. Working to resolve spiritual concerns with some
  4. Multiple visits to hospitals and rehabilitation facilities
  5. Held prayer service for Gospel Meeting
  6. Received report from Rich Dolan's Cambodia mission effort
  7. Held a "Friends and Family Day"
  8. Held a Gospel Meeting with Noel Whitlock
  9. Numerous calls to check on members with concerns
  10. Kenneth Houston to provide security plan for worship services
  11. Build building to secure lawn and maintenance equipment
  12. Cheryl Bode distributed materials on Chimala Mission and hospital
  13. Meeting with new members
  14. Prepare signs for auditorium doors to be left open during class time
  15. Set aside emergency funds to provide financial assistance to members in need
  16. Accepted "Visitation" report from Joe Kelley
  17. Donation from a member for new equipment for building
  18. Signs and pamphlets prepared for gospel meeting
  19. Contacted minister in Huntsville, TX about incarcerated man wanting to be bap-
      tized as a result of World Bible School
  20. Received report from Blane Anderson on the World English Institute
  21. Fall Festival for children
  22. Held Senior's luncheon

- 11.09.2017 - Archer Honea will be going to Chimala to assist with the mission work

- 11.19.2017 - Bridal shower for Bailie Putman

- 12.16.2017 - Carry Conceal Training

- 12.31.2017 - New Year Eve's Party

2018

- 01.08.2018 - Howard Tackett passed away

- 01.19.2018 - Noah Schriner, 17 year old son of Ron and Lorna, died in a car accident.

- 01.28.2018 - Annual corporate meeting after evening services

- 01.28.2018 - The 4th, 5th & 6th Grade class collected $32.93 to help support Joe Kelley's
      trip to the Philippines. Their good hearts and example are an encouragement
      t o us all.

- 02.11.2018 - Visitation Group meets at 4:00

- 02.15.2018 - Young at Heart Fellowship 1:00 p.m.

- 03.01.2018 - Joe Kelley returned to Philippines

- 03.30.2008 - LTC Convention in Rogers, AR

- 03.25.2008 - Audrey Little, daughter of Travis and Brook Little, was baptized into Christ

- 04.07.2018 - Girls' Brunch to honor Makeila Dreiling and Taylor Lee home of Lori Wooten

- 04.09.2008 - Corie Ann Bates put on her Lord in baptism

- 05.06.2018 - Graduating Seniors Displays: Makeila Dreiling and Taylor Lee

- 05.23.2018 - Clothing and More Swap

- 06.01.2018 - Wedding of Kelsey Parrott and Austin LeGrow

- 06.06.2018 - Rich Dolan told about work in Cambodia

- 06.08.2018 - Drew Morris and Sterling LeDoux were baptized into Christ at Burnt Cabin Bible Camp. Drew is granddaughter of Mark Messick; Sterling is son of David & Rebecca LeDoux.

- 06.17.2018 - Class for Young Adults & College Students

- 07.01.2018 - Annual "Independence Day" Fellowship, Feast & Fireworks

- 07.23.2018 - Virgil Harris passed away

- 09.23.2018 - Christina Welch was baptized into Christ following evening service

- 09.29.2018 - Eddie & Linda Bates' 50th Wedding Anniversary Celebration

- 10.07.2018 - Friends & Family Day

- 10.27.18 - Fall Festival

- 12.02.18 - First Sunday Fellowship

- 12.31.18-New Year Eve's Devotion and Fellowship

From the Elders . . .

What a loving, caring congregation we are blessed to shepherd here at Whispering Hills. We thank every member for helping to make the Church of Christ at Whispering Hills a wonderful place to worship and serve our Lord.

As we begin 2019 let us all continue to grow in our faith and raise our children " in the training and instruction of the Lord" (Ephesians 6:4). If we do not attend our Bible classes regularly, we miss an opportunity to grow spiritually. In addition to being a blessing to each of us, Bible class attendance honors our God, honors the efforts of our teachers, and is an encouragement to others. Teachers spend countless hours preparing Bible based material to help in our spiritual growth. All these efforts are to help us and our children find the way to heaven. There are three adult classes (Auditorium, New Addition and a Young Adult/College) and numerous classes for all other ages. Let's all plan on attending these wonderful Bible classes.

Our Sunday and Wednesday evening services provide opportunities for worship, our spiritual growth and fellowship. As the elders of this congregation, it is our scriptural assignment to make sure every member has every opportunity to grow stronger spiritually. We encourage everyone to take advantage of every opportunity to draw closer to God through your Bible Class attendance and our evening services. " Let us not give up meeting together, as some are in the habit of doing...." Hebrews 10:25 "Instead, speaking the truth in love, we will in all things grow up unto him who is the Head, that is Christ. From Him the whole body, joined and held together by every supporting ligament, grows and builds itself up in love as each one does his part." Ephesians 4:15

We pray for our Lord's guidance and blessing as we approach the New Year. We love each and every one of you and appreciate all your efforts in our Lord's kingdom.

In His service,

Mike . Wayne . Steve . Tony

Addendum

The Dream Becomes a Reality by Geames Wooten, published in Vol. 2, No. 3, April 2009, Abundant Living Magazine, Harding University Institute for Church & Family.

Disclaimer: The editor of Abundant Living Magazine added the statement: "At her death the land was deeded to the Broken Arrow Church of Christ with the condition that a church be built there." This was a mistake because Bea and Dan Stackhouse actually deeded the land before they died and actually worshipped with us on September 1, 2002, and again on June 6, 2004, when we worshipped for the first time in the completed building.

The Story of a Church Plant

The Dream Becomes Reality

by GEAMES WOOTEN

Thank God for great men and women of God who dedicate their lives to growing the Kingdom. Thank God for great elders who have a mindset that allows them to see the need for new congregations.

Several years ago, the elders of the Broken Arrow Church of Christ dreamed of establishing another congregation in the area. Nine years ago, a 20-acre tract of land was given to the Broken Arrow Church of Christ for the purpose of establishing a new congregation of the Lord's people in Southeast Broken Arrow.

We had come to know the donor of the 20 acres when we built a home in the country and needed a place to keep our horses. We contacted Bea to ask if we could rent some land for the horses. She declined our request to rent but said we could use the pasture as if it were our own.

Over the next few years, we often visited Bea and her husband. Bea had grown up on the property, and it was her dream when she was a girl that one day there would be a church meeting on her daddy's land. At her death, the land was deeded to the Broken Arrow Church of Christ with the condition that a church be built there. During the elders' planning sessions in 2001 and 2002, a vision was developed for the new congregation.

The first meeting of Take-a-City Group No. 8, the name designated for those interested in helping plant the new congregation, took place in January 2002 at the Broken Arrow church building after evening services.

We began meeting once a month and soon decided on the name, Church of Christ at Whispering Hills, giving Christ the preeminence and the adjoining addition a key to location. We made plans at these meetings and implemented them between

Abundant Living **21**

meetings. Since none of us had been involved in establishing a new congregation, this whole experience was new to us.

On Feb. 14, 2002, the elders of the Broken Arrow church sent a letter to all of its members, outlining plans for the church plant. In the letter, the elders committed to helping fund a minister for the new congregation as of January 2003. As a result, we had to move our plans forward to begin the new congregation sooner than originally planned.

We had worshipped with the Broken Arrow Church of Christ for 38 years. Our children grew up there and were part of that body. It is one of the most well balanced, mission-minded and benevolent churches in existence.

It was difficult for us to leave Broken Arrow, but we were excited about the new work. We had been on several mission trips, and this was kind of like going on a mission trip without having to leave home.

We met for the first time as a new congregation on Sept. 1, 2002, at the Main Place, Broken Arrow's Senior Citizens Center. We had 101 people present, including the core group of 62 from the Broken Arrow church who had committed to moving their membership to Whispering

The Vision

Church of Christ At Whispering Hill
21349 East 111th St Broken Arrow, Ok 74014

Hills. The rest were people from Broken Arrow and surrounding congregations who came to wish us well.

During the two years we met at the Senior Citizens Center, we had to set up chairs, put out song books and make everything ready for class and worship each time. The ladies had classes in the hallways and brought their aids and materials each time. When services were over, everything had to be put away and the building left

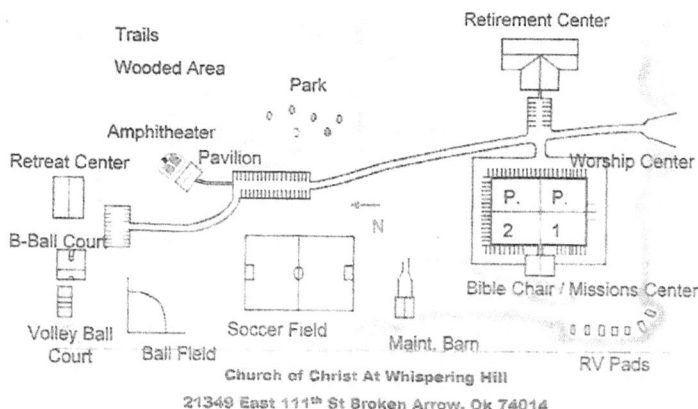

Everyone, including Evan, did his or her part for the church family while they met at the senior citizens center. Putting out songs books and chairs became routine service for all.

clean. We became a close-knit family as we worked together toward our goal.

Early in the process, we decided we would rather build the first phase of our building than have a located preacher. This decision really worked to our advantage because in less than two years, we had our own facility *and* our first minister. Although Broken Arrow did not end up having to furnish Whispering Hills monetary help, they did share their ministers and others who preached for us.

We installed our first elders Oct. 6, 2002. They were Nathan Bell, Jerry Spradley and me. I had been an elder at Broken Arrow for 18 years, and Jerry and Nathan had been deacons for several years. We worked to ensure that we had stable leaders who could keep us focused on God and His Word.

On Jan. 5, 2003, we had the groundbreaking service, and the

22 *Abundant Living*

property was deeded over to Whispering Hills. We had our first worship service June 6, 2004, in our new building. The men of the congregation did much of the work on the property and the building, which saved the church thousands of dollars.

Our first minister, Dan Langdon, who had been a missionary in Scotland, was present for that first meeting, but he and his family were not able to move to Broken Arrow until August.

This experience has taught us that God blesses with success a church that has a vision, goals and dreams and where every member carries his or her load and trusts God for the results. We realize there are many ways to plant a church. This method worked well for us.

It was not our intention to draw Christians from other congregations. The fields were "white unto harvest," and the large part of our growth came from wayward Christians who had not been worshipping anywhere. We now have 251 members, about 30 of whom are new Christians.

On January 8, 2008, Dale and JoAnn Graham, came from Bowling Green, Ky., to work with us. We continue to grow, having around 30 visitors every Lord's Day. We believe our goals, plans, hard work and sound teaching have the attention and blessings of God because many of those who were visiting are now a part of the church family here at Whispering Hills.

Many great blessings have accompanied the establishment of this new congregation. Of course, the greatest blessing of all is the growth of the kingdom of God and the spiritual growth of its people.

We wanted our congregation to be outgoing and friendly to members and visitors alike. We wanted to be a good neighbor in our community. We wanted the community to use our building for meetings, weddings and the like – and they are. We have more than 200 Girl Scouts who use our building and grounds for camp week in June each year. What a blessing as 200 sets of parents and children walk through the doors of the church building every summer.

Age has nothing to do with serving the Lord. Some of our men are over 70 and had never before led a prayer or given a devotional. Now, they are actively participating in leadership roles.

God has blessed each of us with at least one talent. We can all do something to help grow a church – and it can happen right where we are.

Statements of Understanding
Drafted by the Broken Arrow Church of Christ Elders
February 14, 2002
Regarding 111th Property

• Do what we can to ensure the establishment of a doctrinally sound church on the property.
• Do what we can to keep the establishment of the church from being perceived as a split from the Broken Arrow congregation.
• Encourage those who express interest in the project, regardless of their present Church of Christ membership.
• We will not be the oversight eldership of the 111th congregation.
• We will retain ownership of the property until an appropriate time and condition of transfer exists.
• We will encourage the new congregation to make plans for expansion into a congregation of 2,000 or more members because the site will accommodate a large congregation.
• We will remain committed to providing the best possible opportunity for spiritual and numeric growth at our present location while helping a church become established on the 111th property.
• We encourage and will support the establishment of a Bible chair on the 111th property. The new university is growing and establishment of a Bible chair is important.
• Funding and other services by the Broken Arrow congregation will be handled as we currently administer assistance for any mission work.
• Members or staff from our congregation who work on the 111th project will be considered members in good standing who are performing a local mission effort.

www.ingramcontent.com/pod-product-compliance
Lightning Source LLC
Chambersburg PA
CBHW081254040426
42452CB00014B/2502